Mollie MAKES CROCHET

20+ CUTE PROJECTS FOR THE HOME PLUS HANDY TIPS AND TECHNIQUES

Contents

Get hooked!

Crochet—a little bit retro, a little bit thrifty looking—it seems to sum up the modern handmade, homespun look we creatives love so much. You can search high and low for that just-right granny blanket, or you can go ahead and learn this enjoyable and highly addictive technique and make it yourself (we strongly advise the second option!). Choosing your pattern and your yarns is just as much fun as getting cozy in front of the TV for some me-time crafting. And the thrill of making something beautiful that you'll forever feel proud of? Well, we all know you can't beat that feeling.

So, we're so excited to present this crochet guide—full of easy to follow instructions and fresh projects from all our favorite *Mollie Makes* designers, from Emma Lamb to Anita Mundt. Let these talented hooksters share their years of experience, handy tips and anecdotes with you.

Having recently got to grips with the basics myself, I'll be reading along with you.

Lara

Lara Watson
Editor, *Mollie Makes*

Patterns

Working from patterns

Crochet patterns come in two main types: the written kind, where the rows or rounds needed to complete the project are typed in word form; and charts or graphs, which rely on the reader following a schematic drawing. Some patterns will provide both of these options.

READING A WRITTEN PATTERN

So as not to take up a huge amount of space, written patterns use standardized terminology along with characters such as parentheses, brackets, and asterisks to denote repeated instructions. Read through the whole pattern before you begin— knowing what comes next will often help you avoid making a mistake when following the instructions.

SQUARE BRACKETS [ ]

Square brackets are used when an instruction needs to be repeated or where more than one stitch needs to be worked into the same stitch or place.

ASTERISKS *

These are sometimes used in place of, or can be written in conjunction with, square brackets. The most common place to find an asterisk is in a command such as "rep from *", which would mean that you find the first asterisk above this instruction and repeat the section of pattern from this point. Sometimes asterisks are used in pairs, for example "rep from * until **", which would mean that the pattern is repeated from the first single asterisk above the instruction to the following double pair. Be careful to make sure you are working from the correct asterisk; some patterns use them throughout, so you could be in danger of following the repeat from the wrong asterisk. Always search for the first asterisk before the instruction.

PARENTHESES ( )

Parentheses are used to give you an extra written instruction, such as (counts as a stitch) or (20 stitches made). Parentheses are also commonly used to tell you the stitch count at the end of a row or a round.

CAPITAL LETTERS

Capital letters are often used in place of a color name to save space, or to avoid confusion in case you decide to make the project in an alternative colorway. Colors may be listed in alphabetical order: A, B, C; or you may be given abbreviations, such as MC (for "main color") and CC (for "contrast color"). The letter used to describe the yarn will be listed alongside the yarn name in the materials list at the beginning of the pattern.

ABBREVIATIONS

Written patterns contain many abbreviations. These can differ depending on whether you are following a U.S. or U.K. pattern; always check the given abbreviations to make sure that you have understood the instruction. U.S. terms have been used for the patterns in this book, although U.K. equivalent terms are included in the techniques section. For stitch abbreviations see also page 87.

beg	begin(s); beginning	MB	make bobble
CC	contrast color	MC	main color
ch	chain	mm	millimeter(s)
ch-sp	chain space	rem	remain(ing)
cm	centimeter(s)	RS	right side
corner-sp	corner space	sc	single crochet
dc	double crochet	sc2tog	single crochet two stitches together (decrease by one stitch)
dc2tog	double crochet two stitches together (decrease by one stitch)	sp(s)	space(s)
dec	decrease	sl st	slip(ped) stitch
DK	double knit (yarn weight)	st(s)	stitch(es)
		tr	treble
dtr	double treble crochet	WS	wrong side
g	gram(s)	yd	yard(s)
hdc	half double crochet	yo	yarn over
inc	inc	"	inch(es)

Example:

50g balls (170 yards/155 meters) of Mohair, three in Pink #328 (MC) and one in #301 Blue (CC)

This could also be written as:

50g balls (170 yards/155 meters) of Mohair, three in Pink #328 (A) and one in #301 Blue (B)

Notes

Since some stitch names are the same in both U.S. and U.K. terminology, it can be hard to know which terms a pattern from an unknown source is written in. Keep a look out for "single crochet" or "half double crochet" as these only exist in U.S. terminology. If the pattern includes charts, the problem is resolved since chart symbols are universal—see pages 8–9.

WORKING FROM CHARTS

Reading a chart can take a little practice to get to grips with, especially if you have become used to working from a written pattern. However, the advantage of charts is that they take up a lot less space on the page, and give you a clear visual idea of how the crochet piece will turn out.

Notes

As with abbreviations and terminology, the symbols used can vary from pattern to pattern, so check the chart key to make sure that you have fully understood the instructions.

RECOGNIZING GROUPS OF STITCHES

You may notice that some symbols are grouped to form "V" shapes. These indicate a group of stitches that need to be worked into the same stitch or space. They will increase the number of stitches over a given distance.

The stitch symbols below indicate that either 2, 3, 4, or 5 stitches should be worked into one stitch or space on the previous row. Some may denote a special stitch, such as a shell stitch.

A "tent" shaped group of symbols (Λ) indicates a series of stitches that are partially worked into a range of positions and are then completed by drawing yarn through all the loops on the hook. The stitches are gathered together. They will decrease the number of stitches over a given distance.

The stitch symbols below indicate that either 3, 4, or 5 stitches need to be worked together. These symbols are found when working a pattern such as a chevron.

MOST COMMONLY USED STITCH SYMBOLS

Below is a chart showing the symbols for the most commonly used stitches.

Some other symbols that you may encounter in crochet patterns are included below and right as a useful reference when working from charts.

Chain	O
Slipped stitch	●
Single crochet (U.K. double crochet)	+
Half double crochet (U.K. half treble crochet)	T
Double crochet (U.K. treble crochet)	Ŧ
Treble or triple crochet (U.K. double treble crochet)	Ŧ
Double treble crochet (U.K. treble treble, also referred to as triple treble)	Ŧ

BOBBLES, CLUSTERS, AND POPCORNS

3   4   5

The stitch symbols for these stitches portray an increase and then a decrease of stitches, and mimic the appearance of the stitches themselves. Some bobble and cluster symbols can look very similar, but a popcorn will usually have an oval shape at the top to denote its open end.

PICOTS

Picots are shown by a group of chain stitches (the example left shows 4 chains) joined with a slipped stitch. The number of chains can vary depending upon the pattern.

BULLION STITCH

The symbol for bullion stitch is a long line with a semicircle half way down. Do not confuse this with the symbol for raised stitches, which shows the semicircle at the bottom of the line.

CROSSED STITCHES

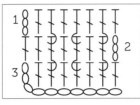

Symbols that intersect indicate a pair or group of crossed stitches. The examples above show a pair of stitches crossed; one stitch crossed over a pair, and a pair crossed over with a chain in between.

SPIKE STITCHES

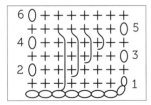

Vertical lines traveling down from a row of stitching indicate where the hook should be placed to create the spike stitch.

RAISED STITCHES

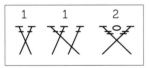

Raised stitches are made by working around the post made by a previous stitch. A raised stitch is indicated by a vertical line with a curved end.

If the open end is to the left, then a raised stitch will be created on the side being worked—the front post.

If the open end is to the right, then a raised stitch will be created on the reverse of the side being worked—the back post.

BACK/FRONT LOOP

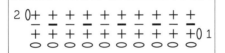

The symbol for working into the back side of the chain that runs along the top of your working fabric is a dark horizontal line. The symbol for working into the front side of the chain is a lightweight line.

Back and front loops may also be represented by half ovals. If the open side is to the bottom, only the back loop is worked; if the open side is to the top, only the front loop is worked.

CURVED AND DISTORTED SYMBOLS

In order to achieve the shape of the finished crochet piece, the symbols often need to be distorted or drawn on a curve instead of in a straight line. In addition, sometimes a complex detail may be drawn to one side with an arrow indicating its position.

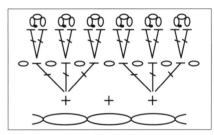

A chart may show extra-large oval chain symbols, for example, so that there is enough space for all the symbols, and therefore all the stitches, required by the design.

ADDITIONAL SYMBOLS

Arrows and numbers may be used to indicate which direction to work and what row or round number is being worked. The chart may have a symbol for joining in a new color, or may be printed in more than one color to make the change obvious.

Gauge

The size of crochet stitches is described as the "gauge" (the U.K. term is "tension") to which they are worked. Gauge must be checked carefully before starting a design as only the gauge/tension will ensure the correct size of the finished piece.

WORKING A GAUGE SWATCH

In a crochet pattern, gauge is usually expressed as the number of stitches and rows found in a section of the fabric—generally a 4" (10 cm) square. In some cases you may be asked to count pattern repeats within a set area rather than individual stitches, but either way the crochet pattern should give you an ideal gauge. It is advisable to work a few more stitches and rows than the pattern gauge instruction suggests, so a true gauge is achieved within the square.

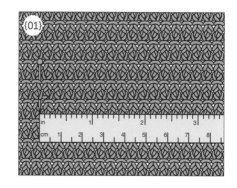

Using the correct hook, yarn and stitches for the project, make a gauge swatch, then use a metal ruler to measure 4" (10 cm) horizontally across the square. Mark this length with a pin at each end.

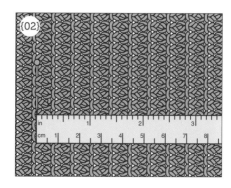

Do the same vertically. Count the number of stitches and rows between the pins.

Notes

When you measure your gauge swatch, try using dressmaking pins with colorful bobble ends; normal pins may get lost amid the crochet stitches and make it hard for you to measure accurately.

ADJUSTING GAUGE

If you find that you have more rows or stitches than the pattern suggests, then your gauge is too tight and you should switch to a larger hook. If there are fewer stitches or rows, then try switching to a smaller size hook. Continue making swatches until you achieve the correct number of stitches to match the gauge.

FANCY STITCH PATTERNS

Measuring over a pattern follows the same principle.

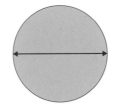

MEASURING A BLOCK

The gauge of a motif or block is usually taken once the piece has been finished and blocked or steamed. Because you can achieve various motif/block shapes with crochet, you will need to be aware of how they should be measured.

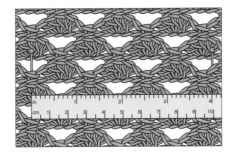

Circular block
Measure straight across the diameter.

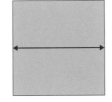

Square block
Measure straight across the center.

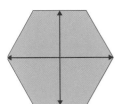

Hexagonal block (six sides)
Measure across the widest point—this is point to point—or from side to side, depending on which your pattern requires.

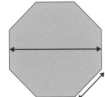

Octagonal block (eight sides)
Measure from side to side, or across one edge, depending on which your pattern requires.

Triangular block
Measure straight across the base.

For the Sunburst motif cushion (pages 48–51), measure straight across the center to check the gauge of the motif.

Contrast-trim pocket placemats

Give your dining table a cheerful retro look with these coordinating placemats, complete with a handy pocket to keep the cutlery in one place. Here four different colors are used in a fresh palette, and the look is kept crisp with a contrasting white border. You could make all the placemats in one color if you prefer.

MATERIALS

50g balls (145 yards/133 meters) of Annell Rapido, two balls in each MC (Pink #3277, Yellow #3215, Light cyan #3222, and Light green #3223), plus one ball in CC (White #3260), or similar yarn (DK, #3 light)

Crochet hook, size E4 (3.5 mm)

Tapestry needle

Sewing needle

Sewing thread in co-ordinating color(s)

SIZE

Placemat: 17" × 12¼" (43 × 31 cm)
Pocket: 4" × 4" (10 × 10 cm)

GAUGE

16dc (8 V-stitch groups) and 10 rows to 4" (10 cm) square using E4 crochet hook.

FEATURED TECHNIQUES

- Working rows of double crochet (page 97)
- Working into chain spaces (page 125)
- Skipping stitches (page 124)
- Creating a crochet edge on a crochet fabric (page 130)

BEFORE YOU BEGIN

The main stitch pattern of the placemats is the V-stitch, formed by working [1dc, 1ch, 1dc] all into the same space.

Turn the work at the end of each row using 3ch as the turning chain.

V-stitch pattern

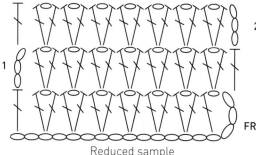

Reduced sample

METHOD

{01} Make the placemats

Foundation row: With MC of your choice, make 68ch (64ch for foundation ch, plus 4ch counts as 1dc plus 1ch), 1dc in fifth ch from hook, skip 1ch, [1dc, 1ch, 1dc into next ch, skip 1 ch] until last ch, 1dc in last ch, turn. (31 V-stitch groups of [1dc, 1ch, 1dc] plus 1dc = 63 sts)

Row 1: 3ch (counts as 1dc), [1dc, 1ch, 1dc] in every ch-sp of previous row until last ch-sp, 1dc into third of 4ch of foundation row (on subsequent rows, make 1dc into third of 3ch of previous row), turn. (30 V-stitch groups of [1dc, 1ch, 1dc] plus 1dc at each end of the row = 62 sts)

Rep row 1 a further 28 times (total of 30 rows). Fasten off yarn and weave in ends.

{02} Make the edging

With CC, join yarn to top right-hand corner and work 2ch (counts as 1hdc) and 3hdc into the corner-sp. Make the edging by working 2hdc into every ch-sp on the top edge. On the two shorter edges, work 2hdc into the space between the 1dc or 3ch and the first V-stitch on every row; on the bottom edge, work 2hdc between each V-stitch group. Work 4hdc into the three other corners, and finish the edging by joining with sl st into the second of the initial 2ch. Fasten off yarn and weave in ends.

{03} Make the pocket

Foundation row: With MC, make 22ch (18ch for foundation ch, plus 4ch counts as 1dc plus 1ch), 1dc in fifth ch from hook, skip 1ch, [1dc, 1ch, 1dc into next ch, skip 1 ch] until last ch, 1dc in last ch, turn. (8 V-stitch groups of [1dc, 1ch, 1dc] plus 1dc = 17 sts)

Row 1: 3ch (counts as 1dc), [1dc, 1ch, 1dc] in every ch-sp of the previous row until last ch-sp, 1dc into third of 4ch of foundation row (on subsequent rows, make 1dc into third of 3ch of previous row), turn. (7 V-stitch groups of [1dc, 1ch, 1dc] plus 1dc at each end of row = 16 sts)

Rep row 1 a further eight times (total of ten rows).
Break MC and join CC.

Row 11: 2ch (counts as 1hdc) and 1hdc into first ch-sp, [2hdc in every chain-sp of previous row]. (8 groups of 2hdc) Fasten off yarn and weave in ends.

{04} Join the pocket to the placemat

Place the bottom edge of the pocket level with the fourth row from the bottom of the placemat, two groups of V-stitch in from the right edge. Using sewing thread in a color that matches the MC, sew the pocket to the placemat along three edges, leaving the upper part open.

ILARIA CHIARATTI

Italian-born Ilaria has lived in the Netherlands with her husband since 2009. She shares her inspiration for interior styling and her crochet work on her blog at www.idainteriorlifestyle.com. She works as a freelance photographer for interiors and runs her own company, IDA Interior LifeStyle, an interior design consultancy.

Crochet Story

I often invite friends over for
Sunday brunch, as we love
to chat and cook together.
I thought these placemats
would be an ideal way to
brighten up our meal. I made
four different colors so various
friends could each decide on
their favorite. The placemats
are made in acrylic yarn, so are
machine-washable, and the
detail of the cutlery-holding
pocket is also practical.

Bouquet of flowers

Flowers are sure to become your favorite motifs to crochet—not just because they are fun and quick, but also because they are so versatile. Whether you crochet each petal and leaf individually to use for appliqué, or you create more realistic three-dimensional motifs, they can be used to decorate anything from blankets to a small girl's dress or a handbag.

MATERIALS

For details of yarns used, refer to the method for each flower on the following pages

Crochet hooks, size B1/C2 (2.5 mm) and size C2 (3 mm)

Tapestry needle

GAUGE

Accurate gauge is not essential for these projects.

FEATURED TECHNIQUES

- Working in the round (page 102)
- Making a ring using a chain (page 102)
- Working stitches into the center of the ring (page 103)
- The magic loop method of starting a round (page 104)
- Increasing around the ring (page 106)
- Joining in new yarn (page 107)
- Working a multicolor motif (page 107)
- Making cluster stitches (page 120)
- Working into chain spaces (page 125)

Crochet Story

Designing and crocheting flowers is an exciting process, offering endless possibilities of shape, color and stitch combinations. For these decorative flowers, I worked with a palette of pink and orange mixed with neutral tones of gray and cream. For the flower motifs themselves, I just picked up my hooks and started creating stitches. Sometimes the freedom of designing without a plan can lead to some very pretty results.

METHOD: RUFFLE CORSAGE

YARN REQUIREMENTS

50g balls (170 yards/155 meters) of DMC Natura Just Cotton, one in each of Ivory #02 (A), Sable #03 (B), Terracotta #40 (C), and Rose Layette #06 (D), or similar yarn (Sport, #2 fine)

SIZE (IN DIAMETER)

3" (7.5 cm)

This is a fresh take on the traditional Irish Rose motif. The design is built up in stages using three rounds of different-colored petals. Each stage of adding petals creates a pretty flower in its own right.

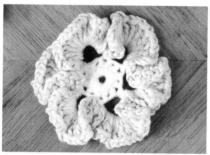

{01} Make the flower

Base ring: With yarn A and C2 hook, 5ch, sl st to form ring.

Round 1: 3ch (counts as 1dc), 11dc into ring, sl st into third of 3ch. (12dc)

Round 2: 1ch, 1sc into same sp as joining sl st, [5ch, skip 1 st, 1sc into next st] five times, 5ch, sl st into first sc. Fasten off.

Layer 1: With yarn B, join yarn in any 5ch-sp, *4ch (counts as 1dc and 1ch), [1dc, 1ch] twelve times into same ch-sp, 3ch, sl st into same ch-sp, sl st into next ch-sp, rep from * five times (makes six petals). Fasten off.

Layer 2: With yarn C, working behind first round of petals, join yarn onto base chain between sixth and seventh dc of any petal, 8ch, [1hdc between sixth and seventh dc of next petal, 6ch] five times, sl st into second of 8ch, *sl st into next ch-sp, 4ch (counts as 1dc and 1ch), [1dc, 1ch] 16 times into same ch-sp, 3ch, sl st into same ch-sp, rep from * five

times (makes six petals). Fasten off.

Layer 3: With yarn D, working behind first round of petals, join yarn onto base chain between eighth and ninth dc of any petal, 10ch, [1hdc between eighth and ninth dc of next petal, 6ch] five times, sl st into second of 10ch, *sl st into next ch-sp, 4ch (counts as 1dc and 1ch), [1dc, 1ch] 21 times into same ch-sp, 3ch, sl st into same ch-sp, rep from * five times (makes six petals). Fasten off. Weave in loose ends.

EMMA LAMB

Emma Lamb is a textile designer and blogger based in Edinburgh, Scotland. Color is her greatest inspiration and she searches endlessly for beautiful palettes to work with. Muted vintage tones and retro combinations are among her favorites, and she adores all things "granny chic." Visit her blog to find out more: emmallamb.blogspot.co.uk.

METHOD: APPLIQUÉ FLOWER

YARN REQUIREMENTS

100g balls (306 yards/280 meters) of DMC Petra 3 Crochet Cotton, one in each of Beige #5712 (A), Gray #5646 (B), and Salmon pink #5352 (C), or similar yarn (Fingering, #1 super-fine)

SIZE (IN DIAMETER)

Rounded petal appliqué flower: 3½" (9 cm)

Pointed petal appliqué flower: 4" (10 cm)

This design features three very simple crochet motifs that could be combined in different ways to create a range of pretty floral patterns for appliqué.

{01} Make the pointed petal flower center

Round 1: With yarn A and B1/C2 hook, make a magic loop, 1ch, 1sc, 7hdc into ring, close ring.

Round 2: Inc by working 2hdc into each of next 8 sts, 1hdc, 1sc, join round with sl st. Fasten off.

Round 3: With yarn B, join yarn in any st, 1ch, [1sc into next st, 2sc into next st] eight times, sl st into first sc, fasten off.

{02} Make the pointed petals (make 7)

With yarn C, 13ch, starting in second ch from hook work 1sc, 1hdc, 1dc, 6tr, 1dc, 1hdc, 1sc over 12ch; for pointed tip work 3ch and 1sc into first of these 3ch; turn and work second half of petal with 1sc, 1hdc, 1dc, 6tr, 1dc, 1hdc, 1sc over 12ch, fasten off.

{03} Make the rounded petal flower center

Work as for pointed petal flower, with yarn A for rounds 1–2 and yarn C for round 3.

{04} Make the rounded petals (make 9)

With yarn A, 9ch, starting in second ch from hook work 3sc, 2hdc, 2dc over 7ch; for rounded tip work 9dc into last ch; work second half of petal with 2dc, 2hdc, 2sc, sl st, fasten off.

{05} Finish the flowers

Weave in loose ends. Find the perfect project to appliqué your finished flowers to.

METHOD: FOLK DAISY

YARN REQUIREMENTS
50g balls (170 yards/155 meters) of DMC Natura Just Cotton, one in each of Rose Layette #06 (A), Safran #47 (B), and Ivory #02 (C), or similar yarn (Sport, #2 fine)

SIZE (IN DIAMETER)
2½" (6.5 cm)

{01} Make the flower
Base ring: With yarn A and C2 hook, 6ch, sl st to form ring.
Round 1: 3ch (counts as 1dc), 15dc into ring, sl st into third of 3ch, fasten off. (16dc)
Round 2: With yarn B, join yarn in any st, 1ch, 2sc in every st (32sc), sl st into first sc, fasten off.
Round 3: With yarn C, join yarn in any st, [5ch, 3dtr cluster over next 3 sts, 5ch, sl st into next st] eight times (makes eight petals); work last sl st into same sp as you joined yarn C, fasten off. Weave in loose ends.

Right: The height of the white petals in this design is created by working double treble stitches (see page 99).

METHOD: LOOPY PETALS

YARN REQUIREMENTS
50g balls (170 yards/155 meters) of DMC Natura Just Cotton, one in each of Rose Layette #06 (A), Agatha #44 (B), and Terracotta #40 (C), or similar yarn (Sport, #2 fine)

SIZE (IN DIAMETER)
2¾" (7 cm)

{01} Make the flower
Base ring: With yarn A and C2 hook, 8ch, sl st to form ring.
Round 1: 3ch (counts as 1dc), 21dc into ring, sl st into third of 3ch,

Right: This flower is crocheted with one central motif with two rounds of different-colored loopy petals added separately.

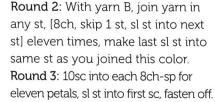

fasten off. (22dc)
Round 2: With yarn B, join yarn in any st, [8ch, skip 1 st, sl st into next st] eleven times, make last sl st into same st as you joined this color.
Round 3: 10sc into each 8ch-sp for eleven petals, sl st into first sc, fasten off.
Round 4: With yarn C, working behind first round of petals, join yarn in any unused st of pink center, [12ch, sl st into next free st of pink center] eleven times, make last sl st into same st as you joined this color.
Round 5: [5sc, 5hdc, 5sc] into each 12ch-sp for eleven petals, sl st into first sc, fasten off. Weave in loose ends.

METHOD: TROPICAL BLOOM

YARN REQUIREMENTS
100g balls (306 yards/280 meters)
of DMC Petra 3 Crochet Cotton,
one in each of Orange #5722 (A),
Beige #5712 (B), Pale lemon #53901
(C), Green #5907 (D), and Light
green #5772 (E), or similar yarn
(Fingering, #1 super-fine)

SIZE (IN DIAMETER)
2½" (6.5 cm) with leaves 1½" (3.8
cm)

{01} Make the flower

Base ring: With yarn A and B1/C2
hook, 5ch, sl st to form ring.

Round 1: 1ch, 10sc into ring, sl st
into first sc.

Round 2: 6ch, [skip 1 st, 1hdc into
next st, 4ch] four times, sl st into
second of 6ch, fasten off.

Round 3: With yarn B, join yarn in
any ch-sp, 1ch, 8sc into this and
every ch-sp, sl st into first sc.

Round 4: [1ch, 1hdc into same sp as
just worked sl st, inc by making 2hdc
in next 6 sts, 1hdc in next st, 1ch, sl st
into next st] five times, work last sl st
into base of first st of this round, (this
sets the start of each petal), fasten off.

Round 5: With yarn C, work each of
the five petals separately as follows:
join yarn in first hdc of any petal, 1ch,
1hdc into same sp as joined yarn,

[1hdc, 1dc] into next st, inc in next 10
sts using dc sts, [1dc, 1hdc] into next
st, turn. (26 sts for each petal)

Round 6: *1ch, skip first st and work
1sc into next 25 sts, sl st into last st,
rep from * for rem petals, fasten off.
Weave in loose ends.

{02} Make the leaves (make 3)

Make one leaf in yarn D and two
leaves in yarn E, working leaf as for
pointed petal (see page 19).

The three-dimensional effect is created with rows of dense increase stitches,
which makes the crochet curl into a petal shape.

METHOD:
DOUBLE-LAYERED CORSAGE

YARN REQUIREMENTS
100g balls (306 yards/280 meters) of DMC Petra 3 Crochet Cotton, one in each of Beige #5712 (A), Orange #5722 (B), Pale lemon #53901 (C), Pink #5149 (D), Green #5907 (E), and Light green #5772 (F), or similar yarn (Fingering, #1 super-fine)

SIZE (IN DIAMETER)
2½" (6.5 cm) with leaves 1½" (3.8 cm) at longest point

{01} Make the bottom flower motif
Base ring: With yarn A and B1/C2 hook, 5ch, sl st to form ring.
Round 1: 3ch (counts as 1dc), 11dc into ring, sl st into third of 3ch. (12dc)

Round 2: 3ch (counts as 1dc), 1dc into same sp, inc by working 2dc in next 11 sts, sl st into third of 3ch, fasten off. (24dc)
Round 3: With yarn B, join yarn in any st, *8ch, starting in second ch from hook work [1sc, 1hdc, 4dc, 1hdc] over 7ch, sl st into next st of beige center, rep from * 23 times (makes 24 petals) with last sl st into same sp as you joined this color, fasten off. Weave in loose ends.

{02} Make the top flower motif
Base ring: With yarn C, 5ch, sl st to form ring.
Round 1: 6ch, [1tr into ring, 2ch] nine times, sl st into fourth of 6ch, fasten off leaving long enough tail for sewing the two motifs together.
Round 2: With yarn D, join yarn in any 2ch-sp, *6ch, starting in second ch from hook work [1sc, 1hdc, 2dc, 1hdc] over 5ch, sl st into next ch-sp of pale lemon center, work another petal into this same ch-sp (makes 2 petals), rep from * nine times (makes 20 petals), fasten off. Weave in loose ends.

{03} Make up flower
Lay top flower motif on top of bottom flower motif and line up from the center. Using the long tail of thread from the top flower motif, hand-sew the two motifs together with a running stitch at the base of the petals. Fasten off securely and weave in loose ends.

{04} Make leaves (make 3)
Make two leaves in yarn E and one leaf in yarn F, working leaf as for pointed petal (see page 19).

This project is made up of two separate crochet flowers that are layered one on top of the other and sewn together. The right-hand photograph shows the back view.

METHOD: PINWHEEL BLOSSOMS

YARN REQUIREMENTS
50g balls (170 yards/155 meters)
of DMC Natura Just Cotton, one in
each of Terracotta #40 (A), Ivory #02
(B), and Sable #03 (C), or similar
yarn (Sport, #2 fine)

SIZE (IN DIAMETER)
3" (7.5 cm)

**{01} Make the flower centers
(make 3)**
Base ring: With yarn A and C2 hook,
5ch, sl st to form ring.
Round 1: 1ch, 10sc into ring, sl st
into first sc, fasten off.

{02} Make the petals
All petals for these three flowers are
crocheted individually as follows:
Join yarn in any st, 2ch, 3dc into
same sp, turn.
2ch, inc by working 2dc in next
3 sts, turn.
2ch, 6dc, turn.
2ch, dc2tog three times over
6 sts, turn.
2ch, work 3dc-cluster over next 3 sts
to dec to 1 st, 2ch, sl st into same sp
as last dec st. Fasten off and weave
in loose ends.

For five-petal white flower, use yarn B
and make five petals, one into every

second stitch of orange center.
Rep for the five-petal gray flower
using yarn C. For the ten-petal
flower, crochet a petal into every
stitch of the orange center,
alternating between B and C.

Each of the petals in this design is worked
individually; the three-dimensional effect
is created by increasing and decreasing
stitches.

Baby blankets

{ *Tuck a sleepy baby into a cozy blanket embellished with a crochet edging. Choose sweet pastel shades that pick out a color from the pattern of the blanket fabric to create an overall look that is soft and harmonious. These crochet edgings should be simple to make as each of them require only two rounds of crochet.*

MATERIALS
30" × 34½" (76 × 87.5 cm) piece of sturdy cotton fabric (plus piece same size for backing fabric if desired) or ready-made baby blanket ready to be edged

Water-soluble fabric marker

Ruler

Large sharp-tipped chenille or darning needle

50g ball of cotton or cotton-blend Sport (#2 fine) yarn in pastel shade to co-ordinate with the blanket fabric

Crochet hook, size G6 (4 mm)

SIZE
31" × 36¼" (79 × 92 cm), including the edging

GAUGE
Accurate gauge is not essential for these projects.

FEATURED TECHNIQUES
- Sewing blanket stitch around the edge of a fabric (page 135)
- Creating a crochet edge on a woven fabric (page 133)
- Making a shell edging (page 132)
- Making a picot edging (page 133)
- Making mesh stitch (page 126)

BEFORE YOU BEGIN
Designer Beata Batik used fabrics from her existing stash to make the baby blankets for this design. She paired mid-weight cotton or cotton-blend fabrics in vibrant florals, fresh plaids, and lively polka dots with a complementary shade of cotton chenille. She picked the crochet yarn, in Sport (#2 fine) cotton or cotton blends, to tone with both fabrics, creating a color palette that was harmonious and soothing – appropriate for a baby blanket.

Crochet Story

I chose to use cotton and cotton-mix yarns to crochet the edgings as they were an appropriate match for the cotton and cotton-blend fabrics I used to make the blankets; this also makes the blankets washable. The yarns I used include DMC Natura Crochet Cotton, Rowan Fine Milk Cotton (a blend of cotton with milk protein), Debbie Bliss Ecobaby Fairtrade Collection (fairtrade and organic cotton), and Annell Cotton 8.

METHOD

{01} Blanket stitch around the fabric

Place the blanket stitches evenly around the edge of the fabric to ensure that the crocheted edging sits flat and even. You can try to do this by eye, or you can mark the positions for the stitches using a water-soluble marker and a ruler. The marks on these blankets are ½" (12 mm) apart; seventy were placed along the long edges and fifty-eight along the short edges.

You may find it tricky to blanket stitch around the whole piece with one length of yarn, so try doing it in two or three sections with a fresh length of yarn each time.

Thread the yarn through a sharp-tipped darning needle that can easily penetrate the woven fabric. Thread the needle with the yarn, bring the two ends together and make a knot. Move the needle to the center; the needle will now be double-threaded. (Compare with page 135, which shows blanket stitch with a single thread.) Start from a point near the corner so as not to start and finish your stitching right at the corner. Continue making a blanket stitch at each mark, making sure your stitches are neither too tight nor too loose; there should be a little give in the stitching as you will be crocheting through them.

Make sure that the stitches aren't made with twisted yarn. This may seem slow-going because of the

Baby blanket edgings:
- shell *(this page)*
- lattice *(next page, left)*
- picot *(next page, right).*

length of the yarn, but it's well worth the result.

After making the blanket stitch at the last mark before the edge of the next corner, make the next one right at the corner; make this corner blanket stitch go right over the corner point at the edge of the blanket on a diagonal. Pivot your blanket around the corner and make the next blanket stitch at the first mark of the next side of the blanket. Make these two corner blanket stitches slightly looser than the others, as they will hold more crochet stitches than the other blanket stitches along the sides. Continue stitching around the entire woven piece and fasten off the yarn.

{02} Crochet the shell edging

Round 1: Starting close to a corner, join yarn to the top loop of the blanket stitch with a sl st. 1ch, and work 2sc into the same blanket

stitch loop; keep working 2sc into each of the following blanket stitch loops until you reach the first blanket corner. Work with a slightly loose gauge so that your two sc sts span nicely over each blanket stitch loop without any pull. At the first corner, work 4sc in both blanket stitch loops (the two loops separated by the diagonal blanket stitch right at the corner). You should now have 8sc stitches at the corner. Pivot your work and cont working 2dc in all the blanket stitch loops along the sides and 4sc in each of the two blanket stitch loops at the corners until you have worked all the way around. Join to beg of round by making a sl st into the first sc. The total number of sc sts should be divisible by four.

Round 2: *Skip 1sc, work 5dc in next sc, skip 1sc, sl st in next sc, rep from * all around the blanket. When you get to the last shell right before your starting point, work it in the

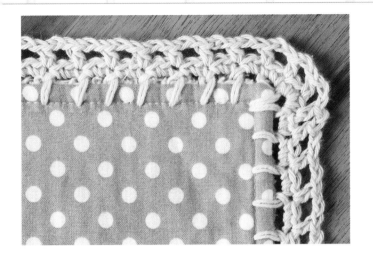

same way as above, except end it by working the sl st into the first sc (of round 1), thereby joining beg of round to the end.
Fasten off and weave in ends.

{03} Crochet the lattice edging
Round 1: Work as for shell edging.
Round 2: 4ch, skip 1sc, work 1hdc in next sc, *2ch, skip 1sc, work 1 hdc in next sc, rep from * all around the blanket. When you get to your last lattice stitch right before your starting point, work it in the same way as above except, instead of making 1hdc, make a sl st into the second ch of the 4ch made at beg of round, thereby joining beg of round to the end.
Fasten off and weave in ends.

{04} Crochet the picot edging
Round 1: Work as for shell edging.
Round 2: 3ch, sl st in first sc, 4ch, sl st in same sc, 4ch, sl st in same sc, 3ch, sl st in same sc, sl st in next 4sc, *3ch, sl st in same sc, 4ch, sl st in same sc, 4ch, sl st in same sc, 3ch, sl st in same sc, sl st in next 4sc, rep from * all around the blanket. When you get to your last set of 4 sl st right before your starting point, work the last sl st into the first sc (of round 1), thereby joining beg of round to the end.
Fasten off and weave in ends.

{05} Pressing to finish
After you finish the edging, if you find that it curls too much for your taste (this may happen particularly with the picot edging), iron it on a low setting so as to define the edging motif better and make it lay flatter. Make sure that the setting on your iron isn't too high, or your yarn may lose its texture. Check beforehand that the yarn may be ironed safely.

BEATA BASIK

Growing up with a seamstress as a grandmother and a crafty grandfather, Beata always loved crafts as a child. Now, as a mother of four, her days are full, but never quite complete unless she dabbles with yarn and fabric. To see where this dabbling leads her, visit her blog Rose Hip (rosehip.typepad.com), or pop by her Etsy shop (www.etsy.com/shop/rosehip).

Three Russian dolls

These three Russian dolls are meant to be displayed together. Their bodies and heads are made in one piece, and are stuffed and weighted at the base so they stand up properly. The shawls and faces are added afterward, with the shawl hiding the color join between the body and the head. Decorative details are made with a slightly smaller hook to keep them neat.

MATERIALS

50g balls (170 yards/155 meters) of DMC Natura Just Cotton, one in each of Aquamarine #25 (A), Passion #23 (red) (B), Topaze #19 (pale pink) (C), Ivory #02 (D), Tournesol #16 (yellow) (F), and Bleu Layette #05 (pale blue) (G), or similar yarn (Sport, #2 fine)

100g ball (473 yards/400 meters) of DMC Petra Crochet Cotton Perle No. 5 in Dark Brown #5938 (E), or similar yarn (Fingering, #1 super-fine)

One skein (9 yards/8 meters) of DMC Mouliné Stranded Cotton in Black #310, or similar (cotton embroidery thread)

Crochet hooks, size B1/C2 (2.5 mm) and C2 (3 mm)

Stitch markers and tapestry needle

Polyester toy stuffing, polypropylene granules, card to fit bases of dolls, PVA glue, old pair of pantyhose

SIZE

Large doll: about 6" (15 cm) tall
Medium doll: about 5½" (14 cm) tall
Small doll: about 4¾" (12 cm) tall

GAUGE

Accurate gauge is not essential for these projects; work to the measurements stated in the pattern.

FEATURED TECHNIQUES

- The magic loop method of starting a round (page 104)
- Making tubular shapes (page 111)
- Working into the back of a stitch (page 119)
- Making a picot edging (page 133)
- Surface embroidery (page 134)
- Surface crochet (page 135)

BEFORE YOU BEGIN

The dolls are made from the base upward. The base is made from a circular piece of crochet and the main part of the body is worked in a spiral.

The work is shaped by sc2tog decreases: work two single crochet stitches together over the next two stitches (decrease by one stitch).

Note that for some instructions you will work into the back loops only (see page 119). This creates a visible ridge on the RS and helps create a good flat base.

Crochet Story

One thing I love about designing decorative items is adding all the details at the end, so I went to town decorating these dolls! It's worth spending extra time on the faces, as they really create the character of the set. I'd recommend leaving all the faces until the end so you can work on them together, and get the proportions looking right. Something that helps the faces look endearing is to space the eyes a little wider than you'd think—try it!

METHOD: LARGE DOLL

{01} Make the head and body

Start by making the base:

With yarn A and C2 hook, 4ch, leaving a 12" (30 cm) long tail of yarn, sl st to first ch to join.

Round 1: 1ch, 6sc into the ring, sl st to first ch to join. (6 sts)

Round 2: 1ch, 2sc into each st, sl st to first ch to join. (12 sts)

Round 3: 1ch, *1sc in next st, 2sc in next st, rep from * five times, sl st to first ch to join. (18 sts)

Round 4: 1ch, *2sc, 2sc in next st, rep from * five times, sl st to first ch to join. (24 sts)

Round 5: 1ch, *3sc, 2sc in next st, rep from * five times, sl st to first ch to join. (30 sts)

Round 6: 1ch, *4sc, 2sc in next st, rep from * five times, sl st to first ch to join. (36 sts)

Round 7: 1ch, *5sc, 2sc in next st, rep from * five times, sl st to first ch to join. (42 sts)

Round 8: 1ch, *6sc, 2sc in next st, rep from * five times, sl st to first ch to join. (48 sts)

Round 9: 1ch, and working in back loops only of the sts of the previous round, work 1sc in each st. Do not close off the round with a sl st.

Make the body:

From now on, do not close off each round with a sl st, but continue working in a spiral. It may help to mark the first st of the round with a stitch marker.

Round 10: (Working in both loops of the st as normal) *2sc in next st, 11sc, rep from * three times. (52 sts)

Rounds 11 and 13: 1sc in each st to end of round.

Round 12: *2sc in next st, 12sc, rep from * three times. (56 sts)

Round 14: *2sc in next st, 13sc, rep from * three times. (60 sts)

Round 15: 1sc in each st to end of round.

Rep round 15 until body measures 1½" (3.5 cm) tall.

Stiffen the base with card:

Cut a circle of card to fit inside the base, and pierce a hole in the center with a needle (see picture below). Stick this circle inside the base of the doll with PVA glue, making sure that the long tail end of yarn is pushed through the center hole to the RS, and not stuck underneath the circle.

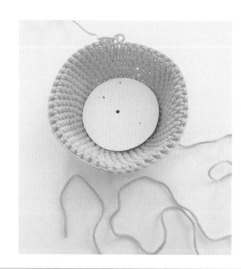

Continue making the body:

Next round: *Sc2tog, 13sc, rep from * three times. (56 sts)

Next round: 1sc in each st to end of round.

Next round: *Sc2tog, 12sc, rep from * three times. (52 sts)

Next round: 1sc in each st to end of round.

**Next round: *Sc2tog, 11sc, rep from * three times. (48 sts)

Next round: 1sc in each st to end of round.

Next round: *Sc2tog, 10sc, rep from * three times. (44 sts)

Next round: 1sc in each st to end of round.

Next round: *Sc2tog, 9sc, rep from * three times. (40 sts)

Next round: 1sc in each st to end of round.

Next round: *Sc2tog, 8sc, rep from * three times. (36 sts)

Next round: 1sc in each st to end of round.** Rep last round twice more. Fasten off.

Secure the weight to stabilize the body:
Pour polypropylene granules into one toe of the pantyhose and tie off to make a ball that will fit inside the body. Using the long tail of yarn attached to the base, thread it onto a tapestry needle and push it through the central hole in the base to the WS (see picture left). Pass it all the way through the center of the ball of granules, and then back through the ball so that both ends emerge in the same place. Push the needle back through the hole in the center of the base piece of card from the inside to the outside. Pull tight so that the ball of granules sits securely on the base, and fasten

off the end of yarn, weaving it in on the base.
Stuff the body firmly with polyester toy stuffing.

Now make the head:
Join yarn B and work 1 round of sc.
Next round: *2sc in next st, 8sc, rep from * three times. (40 sts)
Next round: 1sc in each st to end of round.
Next round: *2sc in next st, 9sc, rep from * three times. (44 sts)
Next round: 1sc in each st to end of round.
Rep last round another three times.
Taking the current start of the round as the "back" of the doll, turn it so that the opposite side is facing for the "front" and mark the central 10 sts across the front with two markers in the first and the tenth st (see picture at left). Work 1sc in each st up to and including the st with the second marker. The next st after the second marker will be the new starting st of the round, so you can remove both markers and replace with one marker in this st to mark the start of the round.
Note that the decreases in the next three decrease rounds are spaced so that the front of the head remains flat: work plain sc over the front 10, and later 9 sts; the other decs are evenly spaced over the rest of the sts.

CARA MEDUS

Cara lives in Bristol, U.K., with her husband and two boys. She loves designing things to knit and crochet, and occasionally finds some time to do a bit of illustration and papercraft. Her other passions are cake and coffee! www.caramedus.com

Next round: Sc2tog, 9sc, sc2tog, 8sc, sc2tog, 9sc, sc2tog, 10sc. (40 sts)

Next round: 1sc in each st to end of round.

***Next round: *Sc2tog, 5sc, rep from * three times, sc2tog, 10sc. (35 sts)

Next round: 1sc in each st to end of round.

Next round: *Sc2tog, 4sc, rep from * three times, sc2tog, 9sc. (30 sts)

Next round: 1sc in each st to end of round.

Next round: *Sc2tog, 3sc, rep from * five times. (24 sts)

Next round: *Sc2tog, 2sc, rep from * five times. (18 sts)

Stuff the body firmly.

Next round: *Sc2tog, 1sc, rep from * five times. (12 sts)

Next round: [Sc2tog] six times. (6 sts)

Fasten off, leaving a long tail of yarn. Finish stuffing and use tail end of yarn to sew up the remaining hole. Weave in ends.***

{02} Make the shawl

Worked from top to bottom.

With yarn B and C2 hook, make 36ch loosely.

Row 1: (WS) 1sc in each ch, beg with the 2nd ch from hook, turn. (35 sts) Check that this row fits around the neck of the doll with a gap equal to about 2 sts at the front when pulled tight. If it is too short, work the foundation chain more loosely, or go up a hook size to E4 (3.5 mm).

Row 2: 1ch, *8sc, 2sc in next st, rep from * twice, 8sc, turn. (38 sts)

Rows 3, 5, 7, 9 and 11: 1ch, 1sc in each st to end, turn.

Row 4: 1ch, *9sc, 2sc in next st, rep from * twice, 8sc, turn. (41 sts)

Row 6: 1ch, 10sc, 2sc in next st, [9sc, 2sc in next st] twice, 10sc, turn. (44 sts)

Row 8: 1ch, *10sc, 2sc in next st, rep from * twice, 11sc, turn. (47 sts)

Dec at either end of the row to shape the corners as follows:

Row 10: 1ch, sc2tog, 9sc, 2sc in next st, [11sc, 2sc in next st] twice, 9sc, sc2tog, turn. (48 sts)

Row 12: 1ch, sc2tog, 9sc, 2sc in next st, [11sc, 2sc in next st] twice, 10sc, sc2tog, turn. (49 sts)

Row 13: 1ch, sc2tog, 1sc in each st to last 2 sts, sc2tog. (47 sts)

Fasten off and weave in ends.

Make an edging for the shawl:

With RS of shawl facing, rejoin yarn B at left-hand end of first row, 1ch and sc evenly down the opening edge, along the bottom and up the other opening edge, working 1sc in each row end and 2sc in each corner st. Fasten off, leaving a long end for sewing the shawl to the body. Before you sew the shawl to the body, work the decoration as set out below.

{03} Make the flowers for the shawl

With yarn C and B1/C2 hook:

1st flower: 3ch, 1dc into the first of these ch (this becomes the center of the flower), 3ch, sl st into the center, *3ch, 1dc into the center, 3ch, sl st into the center, rep from * once to make final petal.

2nd and subsequent flowers: **9ch (joining ch), 1dc into third ch from hook (center), 3ch, sl st into the center, 3ch, 1dc into the center, sl st into the joining ch that is 3ch away from the center, 2sl st along the joining ch toward the center, sl st into the center, 3ch, 1dc into the center, 3ch, sl st into the center. Rep from ** until the strip of flowers is long enough to fit around the edge of the shawl (ten flowers were made).

Fasten off, weave in ends and sew around the edge of the shawl.

Sew the shawl to the body with the opening at the center front, covering the join between the head and body colors.

{04} Make the face

With yarn D and B1/C2 hook, make a magic loop, 1ch and 6sc into the loop. Sl st to the ch at beg of round to join. (6 sts)

For the first few rounds of a small circle it can be difficult to sl st to the first ch of the round to join; you can sl st to the first st of the round instead but remember to work the first st of the round in the same st as the one that you slipstitched to. Cont as for rounds 2–6 of the base of the doll.

Fasten off, leaving a long tail for sewing the face to the head. Pull up the starting tail end as much as possible to close the hole, and then sew any remaining hole closed. Make the following details before sewing the face to the front of the head. Try marking the position of the features with pins before sewing.

Make the mouth:
Split a strand of yarn B in half and use to make 6 small chain stitches (embroidery chain stitch, not crochet) for a mouth.

Make the cheeks (make 2):
Split a strand of yarn C in half, and, with a B1/C2 hook, 2ch, 6sc into the second ch from the hook, sl st to the first st. Fasten off, leaving a long end for sewing to the face. Weave in the starting tail end and sew to the face.

Make the eyes:
With two strands of black embroidery cotton, make a circle of small chain stitches (embroidery) for the eyes.

Use this photograph as a guide for making the facial features of the doll.

{05} Make the hair (make 2 pieces)
With yarn E and B1/C2 hook, 9ch.
Round 1: 2sc (beg in the second ch from the hook), 1hdc, 2dc, 1hdc, 2sc, 2ch, rotate the work 180 degrees to work along the other side of the foundation ch, 2sc, 1hdc, 2dc, 1hdc, 2sc, 1ch, sl st to first st.
Round 2: 1sc in each st along one side of the piece. Sl st to the point at the end.
Fasten off, leaving a long tail of yarn for sewing the hair to the body. Weave in the starting tail end. Position the two hair pieces so that they overlap the join between the face and the head – they will be bigger than the face piece. Sew in place.

{06} Make the flower decoration
Make the yellow petals:
With yarn F and B1/C2 hook, 4ch and sl st to join into a ring.
Round 1: 1ch, 6sc into the ring, sl st to first ch to join. (6 sts)
Round 2: 1ch, *1sc into next st, 6ch, rep from * five times, sl st to first sc of round to join. (6 6-ch loops)
Round 3: [6sc into next ch-loop] six times, sl st to first sc of round to join. Fasten off, leaving a long tail to sew the flower to the body.

Make the brown leaves:
With yarn E and B1/C2 hook, [16ch and sl st into first ch] twice. Fasten off, leaving a long tail to sew the two leaves to the body.

METHOD: MEDIUM DOLL

{01} Make the head and body

Start with the base:
With yarn C and C2 hook, work as for the base of the Large Doll up to and including round 7. (42 sts)
Next round: 1ch, and working in the **back loops only** of the sts of the previous round, work 1sc in each st. Do not close off the round with a sl st.

Make the body:
From now on, do not close off each round with a sl st, but continue working in a spiral. It may help to mark the first st of the round with a stitch marker.

Next round: (Working in both loops of the st as normal) *2sc in next st, 6sc, rep from * five times. (48 sts)
Next round: 1sc in each st to end of round.
Next round: *2sc in next st, 11sc, rep from * three times. (52 sts)
Next round: 1sc in each st to end of round.
Rep last round until the body measures 1¼" (3 cm) tall.

Stiffen the base with card as for the Large Doll.
Cont working body as for the Large Doll from ** to **. (36 sts)
Make a ball of polypropylene granules as for the Large Doll and stuff using polyester toy stuffing.

Next round: *Sc2tog, 7sc, rep from * to end. (32 sts)
Next round: 1sc in each st to end of round.
Next round: *Sc2tog, 6sc, rep from * to end. (28 sts)
Next round: 1sc in each st to end of round.
Rep last round twice.
Fasten off.

Make the head:
Join yarn G and work one round of sc.
Next round: *2sc in next st, 6sc, rep from * three times. (32 sts)
Next round: 1sc in each st to end of round.

Next round: *2sc in next st, 7sc, rep from * three times. (36 sts)
Next round: 1sc in each st to end of round.
Next round: *2sc in next st, 8sc, rep from * three times. (40 sts)
Next round: 1sc in each st to end of round.
Rep last round twice.

Taking the current start of the round as the "back" of the doll, turn it so that the opposite side is facing for the "front" and mark the central 10 sts across the front with two markers in the first and the tenth sts. Work 1sc in each st up to and including the st with the second marker. The next st after the second marker will be the new starting st of the round, so you can remove both markers and replace with one marker in this st to mark the start of the round.
Cont as for head of Large Doll from *** to ***.

{02} Make the shawl
Worked from top to bottom.
With yarn G and C2 hook, make 26ch loosely.
Row 1 (WS): 1sc in each ch beg with second ch from the hook, turn. (25 sts)
Check that this row fits around the neck of the doll with a gap equal to about 2 sts at the front when pulled tight. If it is too short, work the

foundation chain more loosely, or go up a hook size to E4 (3.5 mm).

Row 2: 1ch, *6sc, 2sc in next st, [5sc, 2sc in next st] twice, 6sc, turn. (28 sts)

Rows 3, 5, 7 and 9: 1ch, 1sc in each st to end, turn.

Row 4: 1ch, *6sc, 2sc in next st, rep from * twice, 7sc, turn. (31 sts)

Row 6: 1ch, *7sc, 2sc in next st, rep from * twice, 7sc, turn. (34 sts)

Row 8: 1ch, sc2tog, 5sc, 2sc in next st, [8sc, 2sc in next st] twice, 6sc, sc2tog, turn. (35 sts)

Row 10: 1ch, sc2tog, 6sc, 2sc in next st, [8sc, 2sc in next st] twice, 6sc, sc2tog, turn. (36 sts)

Row 11: 1ch, sc2tog, 1sc in each st to last 2 sts, sc2tog. (34 sts)
Fasten off and weave in ends.

With RS of shawl facing, join yarn A at left-hand end of first row. Work the following picot st along the opening edge, along the bottom and up the other opening edge of the shawl with a B1/C2 hook. Work the sc for each picot st in every alternate st or row end:
1ch, *1sc in next st or row end, 3ch, sl st in first of those 3ch. Rep from * around the edge, working the repeat twice in each corner st. Work 1sc in the last st to finish.
Fasten off, leaving a long end for sewing the shawl to the body.
Before you sew the shawl to the doll's body, work the decoration as follows.

Using a double thread of yarn F, backstitch lines across the shawl and around the head. Space the lines evenly every four rows, using the "holes" between the rows. Work out which rows will have stitching before you start, taking into account where the shawl will join the head. When working on the head, begin and end the rows of stitching at the front, where they will be covered by the face. Do not work a row of stitching on the head any higher than where the join at the front will be hidden by the face and hair.

{03} Make the face

Work the face as for the Large Doll, but work from rounds 2–5 of the base of the Large Doll. Work the mouth and eyes as for the Large Doll, but for the cheeks, use half a strand of yarn C and embroider a circle of chain stitches (embroidery). Try and make the features slightly smaller than those for the Large Doll.

{04} Make the hair (make 2 pieces)

Work as for the hair of the Large Doll, but work round 1 only before fastening off.

{05} Make the decoration

Flowers (make 3):
Round 1: With yarn B and B1/C2 hook, 3ch, 11dc into the first ch, sl st to the top of the 3ch to join.
Fasten off and weave in ends.
Position the three flowers on the body using the photograph below as a guide and hold in place with pins. Use yarn E to sew the flowers to the body with visible straight stitches. Make three long, straight stitches at the base for stems, with a small chain-stitch (embroidery) leaf on each stem.

METHOD: SMALL DOLL

{01} Make the head and body

Start with the base:

With yarn B and C2 hook, work as for the base of the Large Doll up to and including Round 6. (36 sts)

Next round: 1ch, and working in the **back loops only** of the sts of the previous round, work 1sc in each st, sl st to first ch of round to join.

Now make the body:

Work every fourth round in yarn A. Note that with the Small Doll, each round of the body is joined in order to create jogless stripes – unlike the other two doll bodies, which were made in spirals.

Next round: (Working in both loops of the st as normal) 1ch, *2sc in next st, 8sc, rep from * three times, sl st to first ch to join. (40 sts)

Next round: 1ch, 1sc in each st to end of round, sl st to first ch to join.

Next round: 1ch, *2sc in next st, 9sc, rep from * three times, sl st to first ch to join. (44 sts)

Next round: 1ch, 1sc in each st to end of round, sl st to first ch to join. Rep last round until the body measures 1" (2.5 cm) tall.

Stiffen the base with card as for the Large and Medium Dolls.

Next round: 1ch, *sc2tog, 9sc, rep from * three times, sl st to first ch to join. (40 sts)

Next round: 1ch, 1sc in each st to end of round, sl st to first ch to join.

Next round: 1ch, *sc2tog, 8sc, rep from * three times, sl st to first ch to join. (36 sts)

Next round: 1ch, 1sc in each st to end of round, sl st to first ch to join.

Make a ball of polypropylene granules as for the Large Doll and stuff using polyester toy stuffing.

Next round: 1ch, *sc2tog, 7sc, rep from * three times, sl st to first ch to join. (32 sts)

Next round: 1ch, 1sc in each st to end of round, sl st to first ch to join.

Next round: 1ch, *sc2tog, 6sc, rep from * three times, sl st to first ch to join. (28 sts)

Next round: 1ch, 1sc in each st to end of round, sl st to first ch to join.

Next round: 1ch, *sc2tog, 5sc, rep from * three times, sl st to first ch to join. (24 sts)

Next round: 1ch, 1sc in each st to end of round, sl st to first ch to join. Rep last round twice.

Make the head:

From now on, do not close off each round with a sl st, but cont working in a spiral. It may help to mark the first st of the round with a stitch marker.

Join yarn F and work one round of sc.

Next round: 1sc in each st to end of round.

Next round: *2sc in next st, 5sc, rep from * three times. (28 sts)

Next round: 1sc in each st to end of round.

Next round: *2sc in next st, 6sc, rep from * three times. (32 sts)

Next round: 1sc in each st to end of round.

Next round: *2sc in next st, 7sc, rep from * three times. (36 sts)

Next round: 1sc in each st to end of round.

Rep last round.

Taking the current start of the round as the "back" of the doll, turn it so that the opposite side is facing for the "front" and mark the central 8 sts across the front with two markers in the first and the eighth st. Work 1sc in each st up to and including the stitch with the second marker. The next st after the second marker will be the new starting st of the round, so you can remove both markers and replace with one marker in this st to mark the start of the round.

Next round: Sc2tog, 4sc, [sc2tog, 5sc] twice, sc2tog, 4sc, sc2tog, 8sc. (31 sts)

Next round: 1sc in each st to end of round.

Next round: *Sc2tog, 4sc, rep from * three times, sc2tog, 5sc. (26 sts)

Next round: Sc2tog, 3sc, [sc2tog, 2sc] four times, sc2tog, 3sc. (20 sts)

Stuff firmly.

Next round: *Sc2tog, 2sc, rep from * four times. (15 sts)

Next round: *Sc2tog, 1sc, rep from * four times. (10 sts)
Next round: [Sc2tog] five times. (5 sts)

Fasten off, leaving a long tail of yarn. Finish stuffing and use the tail end of yarn to sew up the remaining hole. Weave in ends.

{02} Make the shawl

Worked from top to bottom.
With yarn F and C2 hook, make 22ch loosely.
Row 1 (WS): 1sc in each ch beg with second ch from hook, turn. (21 sts) Check that this row fits around the neck of the doll with a gap equal to about 2 sts at the front when pulled tight. If it is too short, work the foundation chain more loosely, or go up a hook size to E4 (3.5 mm).
Row 2: 1ch, 5sc, 2sc in next st, [4sc, 2sc in next st] twice, 5sc, turn. (24 sts)
Rows 3, 5, 7 and 9: 1ch, 1sc in each st to end, turn.
Row 4: 1ch, [5sc, 2sc in next st] three times, 6sc, turn. (27 sts)
Row 6: 1ch, [6sc, 2sc in next st] three times, 6sc, turn. (30 sts)
Row 8: 1ch, 7sc, 2sc in next st, [7sc, 2sc in next st] twice, 6sc, turn. (33 sts)
Row 10: 1ch, sc2tog, 6sc, 2sc in next st, [7sc, 2sc in next st] twice, 6sc, sc2tog, turn. (34 sts)
Row 11: 1ch, sc2tog, 1sc in each st

to last 2 sts, sc2tog. (32 sts) Fasten off and weave in ends. Work edging as for Shawl of Large Doll using yarn F.

Before you sew the shawl to the body, work the decoration as follows.
With yarn E, work a series of French knots (see page 135) around the edge of the shawl. If you do not want to work French knots, use small beads instead. Sew shawl to body.

{03} Make the face

Work the face as for the Large Doll, but work rounds 2–4 of the base of the Large Doll. Work the mouth and cheeks as for the Medium Doll, but for the eyes, work French knots, or use small beads if preferred. Try to make the features slightly smaller than those for the Medium Doll.

{04} Make the hair (make 2 pieces)

With yarn E and B1/C2 hook, 7ch, sc in second ch from hook, 1hdc, 2dc, 1hdc, 1sc, 2ch, rotate piece 180 degrees to work along the other side of the foundation ch, 1sc in each st along one side of the piece until you reach the point, sl st into the point. Fasten off, leaving a long tail. Weave in short end and sew on as for Large Doll.

{05} Make the decoration

Work round 1 of Flower as for Medium Doll with yarn C, but do not fasten off.
Round 2: *3ch, sl st in st at base of ch, sl st in next st, rep from * to last st, ending with 3ch and sl st in last st. Fasten off, leaving a long tail for sewing, and sew on to body.
With yarn E, work two long chain stitches (embroidery) for leaves, and a couple of straight stitches for the stem. Work a French knot in the center of the flower.

Updated doilies

The single-motif doily, worked in a classic color combination of red, beige, and cream, is a modern take on the traditional white vintage lace doily. The pretty twelve-petal motif used for the coaster set and the multi-motif doily is very versatile: make one motif into a chunky and practical coaster, or, using a single strand of yarn and piecing the motifs together, crochet the doily design.

MATERIALS

Single-motif doily
100g balls (306 yards/280 meters) of DMC Petra 3 Crochet Cotton, one each in Red #5666 (A), Beige #5712 (B), and Cream #53901 (C), or similar yarn (Sport, #2 fine)

Multi-motif doily and coasters
100g balls (306 yards/280 meters) of DMC Petra 3 Crochet Cotton, one in each of Dark gray #5646 (A), Red #5666 (B), Orange #5608 (C), and Pink #5151 (D), or similar yarn (Sport, #2 fine)

Crochet hooks size B1/C2 (2.5 mm) for doilies and E4 (3.5 mm) for coasters

Tapestry needle

SIZE

Single-motif doily:
6¼" (16 cm) in diameter

Multi-motif doily:
9" (23 cm) at widest point

Coasters:
4½" (11.5 cm) in diameter

GAUGE

Accurate gauge is not essential for this project, but may alter the yarn amounts required.

FEATURED TECHNIQUES

Single-motif doily
- Making a ring using a chain (page 102)
- Working stitches into the center of the ring (page 103)
- Working into chain spaces (page 125)
- Creating a crochet edge on a crochet fabric (page 130)

Multi-motif doily and coasters
- Increasing around the ring (page 106)
- Working into chain spaces (page 125)
- Working treble crochet (page 98)
- Joining motifs as you work (page 141)

DESIGNED BY EMMA LAMB

Crochet Story

We all know and love those intricate, vintage white doilies our grannies used to have on every table and under every vase. When designing the multi-motif doily, I wanted to update that traditional white theme by using some intense colors, such as the dark gray, red, and orange, mixed with pink to keep them looking pretty.

METHOD:
SINGLE-MOTIF DOILY

{01} Make the doily

Base ring: Using yarn A and B1/C2 hook, 10ch and sl st to join ring.

Round 1: 3ch (counts as 1dc), 23dc into the ring, sl st into third of 3ch. (24dc)

Round 2: 1ch, 1sc into same sp as joining sl st, [7ch, skip 3 sts of previous round, 1sc into fourth st] five times, 3ch, 1tr into first sc.

Round 3: 1ch, 5sc into stem of 1tr just worked, 9sc into each of next five ch-sps, 4sc into next ch-sp, sl st into first sc.

Round 4: 1ch, 1sc into same sp as joining sl st, [10ch, 1sc into fifth of 9sc of previous round] five times, 10ch, sl st into first sc.

Round 5: 1ch, [1sc into 1sc of previous round, 13sc into ch-sp] six times, sl st into first sc. Fasten off yarn.

Round 6: Using yarn B, join yarn in eighth sc of previous round, 8ch, [skip 5 sts, 1sc into next st, 5ch, skip 5 sts and 1dc into next 3 sts, 5ch] five times, skip 5 sts, 1sc into next st, 5ch, skip 5 sts, 1dc into next 2 sts, sl st into third of 8ch.

Round 7: 3ch, [2dc into ch-sp, 5ch, 1sc into 1sc of previous round, 5ch, 2dc into ch-sp, 3dc] five times, 2dc into ch-sp, 5ch, 1sc into 1sc of previous round, 5ch, 2dc into ch-sp, 2dc, sl st into third of 3 ch.

Round 8: 3ch, 2dc, [2dc into ch-sp, 4ch, 1sc into 1sc of previous round, 4ch, 2dc into ch-sp, 7dc] five times, 2dc into ch-sp, 4ch, 1sc into 1sc of previous round, 4ch, 2dc into ch-sp, 4dc, sl st into third of 3ch.

Round 9: 3ch, 4dc, [2dc into ch-sp, 4ch, 1sc into 1sc of previous round, 1ch, 2dc into ch-sp, 11dc] five times, 2dc into ch-sp, 4ch, 1sc into 1sc of previous round, 4ch, 2dc into ch-sp, 6dc, sl st into third of 3ch.

Round 10: 3ch, 6dc, [2dc into ch-sp, 1ch, 2dc into ch-sp, 15dc] five times, 2dc into ch-sp, 1ch, 2dc into ch-sp, 8dc, sl st into third of 3ch.

Round 11: 3ch, 1dc into each st and ch-sp, sl st into third of 3ch. Fasten off yarn.

Round 12: Using yarn C, join yarn in any st, 1ch and 1sc into same sp, [3ch, skip 2 sts, 1sc into next st] 39 times, 3ch, sl st into first sc.

Round 13: 1ch, [1sc, 1hdc, 2dc, 1hdc, 1sc] into each 3ch-sp, sl st into first sc.

Fasten off yarn and weave in loose ends.

METHOD:
MULTI-MOTIF DOILY
AND TWEEDY COASTERS

{01} Before you begin

Standing stitch is an alternative way of joining a new color. Instead of using chain stitches to begin a round, begin with a new loop on your hook and directly work the stitch. To work a dc, start with a new loop on your hook, yarn over hook, insert hook into work where the stitch is required to pick up your third loop and complete the dc stitch as normal. This means it is easier to disguise the start of a round as there is no telling 3ch.

The coasters are made with two strands of yarn held together. Work the color combinations as follows:
Yarns A and D
Yarns B and D
Yarns C and D

The motifs of the doily are joined together as you go. Work a joining stitch as follows:
Slip working loop off hook, insert hook into 2ch petal point of first motif, put working loop back on hook and pull through petal point, then 1ch.

{02} Make the 12-petal motif for the tweedy coasters

Base ring: Using two yarns held together and E4 hook, *10ch and sl st to join ring.
Round 1: 3ch (counts as 1dc), 23dc, sl st into third of 3ch. (24sts)
Round 2: 5ch (counts as 1dc and 2ch), [skip 1 st of previous round, 1dc into next st, 2ch] until end, sl st into third of 5ch.
Round 3: Sl st into ch-sp, 2ch (counts as 1dc) and 3dc into same ch-sp, 2ch, [4dc, 2ch] into each ch-sp to end, sl st into third of initial 3ch.*
Round 4: Sl st into next 2 sts, [2hdc, 1dc, 1tr, 2ch, 1tr, 1dc, 2hdc] into each 2ch-sp of previous round, sl st into first hdc. (12 petals)
Fasten off and weave in loose ends.

{03} Make the multi-motif doily

Using yarn A and B1/C2 hook, work central motif as for coaster.
Second motif: Using yarn B, work from * to *, and fasten off.
Round 3: Join yarn A and using standing stitch starting technique, 2dc into any ch-sp, 2ch, [4dc, 2ch] eleven times, 2dc into first ch-sp, sl st into first dc.
Round 4: [2hdc, 1dc, 1tr, 2ch, 1tr, 1dc, 2hdc] into each of ten 2ch-sps of previous round (makes ten petals), then work last two joining petals as follows: [2hdc, 1dc, 1tr, 1ch, joining st, 1tr, 1dc, 2hdc], sl st into first hdc. Fasten off and weave in loose ends.
Third motif: Using yarn C for rounds 1–2 and yarn A for rounds 3–4, work as for second motif to last four petals, join ninth and tenth petals to first motif, then eleventh and twelfth petals to second motif.
Fourth–seventh motifs: Rep for fourth motif using yarns D and A, fifth motif using yarns B and A, sixth motif using yarns C and A and seventh motif using D and A; join last six petals to second, first and sixth motifs.

Tweedy coaster

Multi-motif doily

Spike stitch iPad cozy

Crochet is a great way to lend a bit of granny style to your gadgets, and this iPad cozy makes the perfect marriage of retro and modern. The spike stitch pattern looks complicated, but you will soon get the hang of it—the row below will tell you what to do!

MATERIALS

Assortment of DK-weight yarn, with gray as the main color (MC) and eight other vivid colors for the contrast rows—wool, acrylic and cotton will all be suitable. If you are buying yarn specially for the project, you will need one 50g ball of DK (#3 light) yarn in each color

Crochet hook, size C2 (3 mm)

Tapestry needle

SIZE

To fit standard iPad/tablet computer: 8" × 10" (20.5 × 25.5 cm)

GAUGE

5 double clusters and 11 rows to 4" (10 cm) square using C2 crochet hook.

FEATURED TECHNIQUES

- Working double crochet (page 96)
- Working spike stitches (page 115)
- Joining a new yarn (page 100)
- Sewing up seams by oversewing (page 138)

BEFORE YOU BEGIN

If you would like to make this project wider (for a laptop or blanket, for instance), add extra width in multiples of four stitches.

The iPad cozy is crocheted in one piece, then folded in half to form the bottom edge. The two side seams are then sewn together. You could add a button and button loop to the cozy (see pages 141–142) if desired.

The color sequence is random, with the main color, gray, alternating with a vivid color.

Spike Stitch Pattern

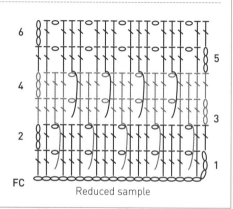

Reduced sample

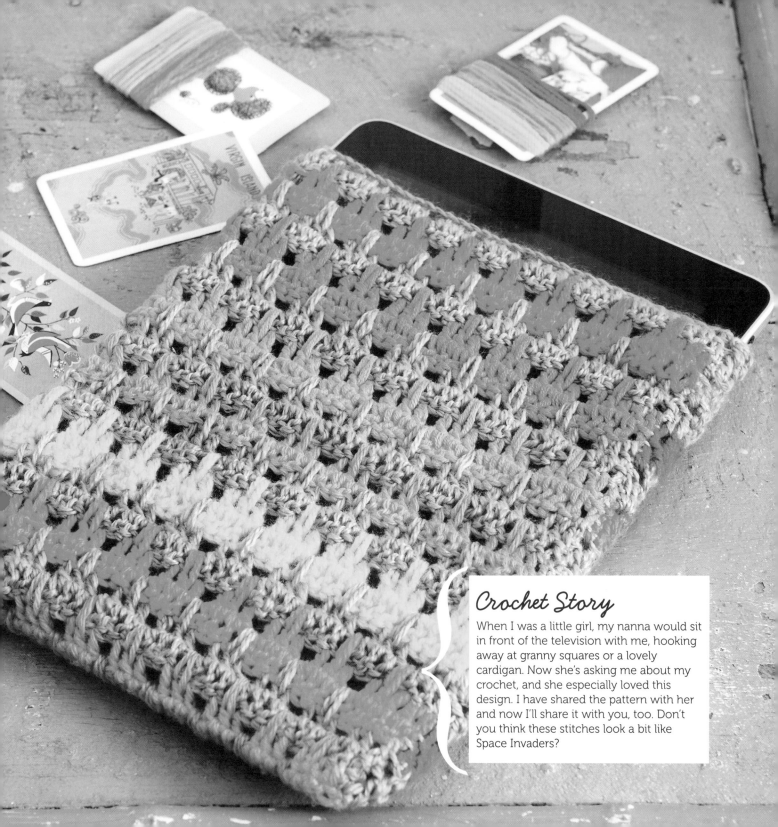

Crochet Story

When I was a little girl, my nanna would sit in front of the television with me, hooking away at granny squares or a lovely cardigan. Now she's asking me about my crochet, and she especially loved this design. I have shared the pattern with her and now I'll share it with you, too. Don't you think these stitches look a bit like Space Invaders?

METHOD

{01} Make the iPad cozy

Foundation chain: Using MC, make ch39 loosely (36ch for foundation chain plus 3ch counts as 1dc).

Row 1: 1dc into fourth ch from hook, *skip 1ch, 1ch, 1dc into each of next 3ch, rep from * seven times, skip 1ch, 1ch, 1dc into each of final 2ch, turn. (You will have ten blocks with a little gap in between each; the clusters at each end are made of 2 sts, while the clusters in between those have 3 sts, and there are nine gaps between the clusters.)

Row 2: 3ch (counts as 1dc), 1dc into next st, *skip next st, 1ch, 1dc into each of next 3 sts, rep from * seven times, skip 1 st, 1ch, 1dc into next st, 1dc into top of 3ch, turn. (This row is the same as row 1 so the blocks of double are now aligned one over the other.) Break yarn, leaving long tail.

Row 3: Join your new color, 3ch (counts as 1dc), 1dc into next st, 1dc into gap between double blocks two rows below (makes spike stitch; you will need to loosen your gauge a bit and it may feel odd making such a long stitch), 1dc into next st (back on the current row again), *1ch, skip next st, 1dc into next st, 1dc into the gap two rows below, 1dc into next st, rep from * six more times, 1ch, skip 1 st, 1dc into next st, 1dc into gap two rows below, 1dc in next st, 1dc in top of 3ch, turn. (You'll now have the beginnings of nine spike stitch clusters. The first and last cluster are made of 4dc as they have an extra fortifying stitch in them; the central seven clusters are made of 3dc with the spike stitch in the center.)

Row 4: 3ch (counts as 1dc), 1dc into each of next 3 sts, *skip 1ch, 1ch, 1dc into next 3 sts, rep from * six more times, skip 1ch, 1ch, 1dc into next 3 sts, 1dc into top of 3ch, turn. Break yarn, leaving long end.

Row 5: Using MC, 3ch (counts as 1dc), 1dc into next st, *skip 1 st, 1ch, 1dc in next st, 1dc into gap two rows below (makes spike stitch), 1dc into next st (back on current row), rep from * seven times, skip 1 st, 1ch, 1dc into next st, 1dc into top of 3ch, turn.

Row 6: 3ch (counts as 1dc), 1dc into next st, *skip 1ch, 1ch, 1dc into each of next 3 sts, rep from * seven times, skip 1ch, 1ch, 1dc into next st, 1dc into top of 3ch, turn. Break yarn, leaving long end.

Rep rows 3–6 until your piece measures 20" (50 cm). Use a new color for each repetition of rows 3 and 4, while rows 5 and 6 are always worked in MC. (This design was made with 54 rows but this may vary depending on what yarn you use.)

{02} Make up the iPad cozy

Fold cozy in half with RS together, matching all edges neatly. Thread your tapestry needle with about 15¾" (40 cm) of yarn. Beg at the top matched edges, oversew down each side, matching the rows neatly as you stitch to the bottom. Rep for other side. Weave in all the loose ends with yarn needle. Turn right way out and tuck your iPad inside.

PIP LINCOLNE

Pip Lincolne lives in Australia. She has written quite a few craft books and blogs about life and happy things at www.meetmeatmikes.com.

Pip loves to crochet, make delicious food, and hang out with interesting people. She chats about craft on Australian television and radio, and runs the annual Softies For Mirabel toy drive, collecting handmade soft toys for the kids the Mirabel Foundation supports.

Wave stitch chair runner

} *This stitch is a softer-edged version of the chevron stitch (see pages 76 and 116). It is worked in a similar way, using pairs of increases and decreases to create "hill" tops and "valley" bottoms. The design is based on pattern repeats, so is easily adapted. For example, you could make it narrower for a scarf or broader to make a blanket or throw.*

MATERIALS

50g balls (93 yards/85 meters) of Rowan Handknit Cotton, two balls in each of Ecru #251 (A), Burnt (dark red) #343 (D), Ochre #349 (E), Raffia (olive green) #330 (F), and Rosso (red) #215 (G), and one ball in each of Cloud (duck-egg blue) #345 (B) and Ice Water (gray-blue) #239 (C), or similar yarn (DK, #3 light)

Crochet hook, size 7 (4.5 mm)

Tapestry needle

SIZE

About 17¾" × 61¼" (45 x 155.5 cm)

GAUGE

Accurate gauge is not essential for this project.

FEATURED TECHNIQUES

- Making wave stitch (page 118)
- Increasing stitches within a row (page 112)
- Decreasing stitches within a row (page 113)
- Joining a new yarn (page 100)
- Blocking a finished crochet piece (page 137)

BEFORE YOU BEGIN

The wave pattern is based on a 16-stitch repeat worked over 14ch/sts.

The color sequence is as follows:

Yarn A
Yarns B and C (used alternately)
Yarn D
Yarn E
Yarn F
Yarn G

Wave pattern

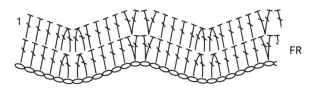

Sample shows two complete waves

METHOD

{01} Make the chair runner

Foundation row: With yarn A, make 73ch (70ch for foundation ch plus 3ch counts as 1dc), 1dc into fourth chain from hook, 1dc into each of next 4ch, [dc2tog over next 2ch] twice, 1dc into each of next 4ch, *[2dc into next ch] twice, 1dc into each of next 4ch, [dc2tog over next 2ch] twice, 1dc into each of next 4ch, rep from * three times, 2dc into final ch, turn. (80dc)

Row 1: 3ch, 1dc into base of 3ch, 1dc in next 4 sts, [dc2tog over next 2 sts] twice, 1dc in next 4 sts, *[2dc into next st] twice, 1dc in next 4 sts, [dc2tog over next 2 sts] twice, 1dc in next 4 sts, rep from * three times, 2dc in top of 3ch from previous row, turn.

Rep row 1, changing the yarn color every two rows following sequence set out in Before You Begin for a total of 98 rows.

Fasten off and weave in all ends and then block the runner.

ANITA MUNDT

Many years ago, Anita studied textile design at Huddersfield University in England, and although she does not work in textiles anymore, she is always creating something in one form or another. Anita lives in a sleepy village in an old schoolhouse, which she and her husband are renovating. Visit her blog at acreativedimension.blogspot.com. Feel free to drop by and say hi!

Crochet Story

My husband has a reading chair that needed a little something to spice it up. I worked this traditional wave stitch pattern into a long runner to give a more masculine feel to the piece, which complements his chair perfectly. Work out a color palette that would suit your taste in décor, and play around with the arrangement—you could make narrower or broader waves, too.

Sunburst motif cushion

This cushion is made up of sunburst motifs. This is a creative way to use up leftover yarn scraps and turn them into something extraordinary, with black used as a unifying color. The back of the cushion is made from one giant granny square, but you could make both sides the same if you prefer.

MATERIALS

50g balls (145 yards/133 meters) of Annell Rapido, four in Black #3259 (A), one in each of Light pink #3233 (B), Fuchsia #3277 (C), and Red #3212 (D), plus small amounts in a variety of vibrant colors for the sunburst motifs, or similar yarn (DK, #3 light)

Crochet hook, size E4 (3.5 mm)

Tapestry needle

Button for fastening, about ¾" (2cm) in diameter

Cushion pad measuring 17¾" × 17¾" (45 × 45 cm) to fit

SIZE

17¾" × 17¾" (45 × 45 cm)

GAUGE

One sunburst motif measures 3⅛" (8 cm) square.

FEATURED TECHNIQUES

- Making clusters (page 120)
- Making a square from a central chain (page 108)
- Joining motifs (pages 139 and 140)
- Crocheting seams together (page 138)

BEFORE YOU BEGIN

You will make thirty-six sunburst motifs in total for the front of the cushion, arranged in six rows of six motifs each to make a square cushion. Each motif consists of three rounds: make rounds 1 and 2 in two different colors of your choice; round 3 is always worked in black.

You can make all the motifs individually and sew them together at the end, or you can join them together as you work.

The back of the cushion is made up of a 19-round granny square with an edging worked in double crochet. You can use the color changes as set out here, or make up your own design.

For back of cushion:

Rounds 1–11: yarn A
Rounds 12–13: yarn B
Rounds 14–15: yarn C
Rounds 16–17: yarn D
Round 18: yarn C
Round 19: yarn B

Crochet Story

Since I started crocheting, more than ten
years ago, I have always used a white
background for my cushions and blankets.
I was curious to see what sort of effect
I could create using a dark background
instead, and this cushion was the result.
Strong, vibrant colors work well set against
black, and the dark background unifies
what could otherwise be a very wide
range of colors.

Sunburst motif: make 36

METHOD

{01} Make the motifs for the front of the cushion (make 36)

Foundation ring: With color 1, 4ch, join with sl st to form a ring.

Round 1: 3ch (counts as 1dc), 11dc into ring, join with sl st into third of 3ch. Fasten off. (12dc)

Round 2: With color 2, 3ch (counts as 1dc), 1dc at base of 3ch, [2dc-cluster in sp between next 2 sts] eleven times, join with sl st into third of 3ch. Fasten off. (12 2dc clusters)

Round 3: Join yarn A to any sp on round 2, 3ch (counts as 1dc), 2dc, 2ch, 3dc all into same sp at base of 3ch to make first corner, *1ch, [3dc into next sp, 1ch] twice, 3dc, 2ch, 3dc into next sp to make next corner, rep from * twice, 1ch, [3dc into next sp, 1ch] twice, join with sl st into third of 3ch. Fasten off and weave in ends. (16 groups of 3dc)

(02) Make the edging for the front

Starting from a corner and with yarn A, work 3ch (counts as 1dc), 2dc, 2ch, 3dc to make the corner. Make the edging by working 1dc into every st, and work the corners as previously set [3dc, 2ch, 3dc], then join with sl st into third of 3ch. Fasten off and weave in ends.

{03} Make the back of the cushion

Foundation ring: With yarn A, 4ch, join with sl st to form a ring.

Round 1: 3ch (counts as 1dc), 2dc into ring, 3ch, *3dc into ring, 3ch, rep from * twice more, join with sl st into third of 3ch.

Round 2: Make 3sl st to reach the corner-sp, 3ch (counts as 1dc), [2dc, 2ch, 3dc] into same sp (corner made), *1ch, [3dc, 2ch, 3dc] into next 3ch-sp; rep from * twice more, 1ch, join with sl st into third of 3ch.

Round 3: Make 3sl st to reach the corner-sp, 3ch (counts as 1dc), [2dc, 2ch, 3dc] into same sp, *1ch, 3dc into 1ch-sp, 1ch, **[3dc, 2ch, 3dc] into next 3ch corner sp; rep from * twice and from * to ** once again, join with sl st into third of 3ch.

Rounds 4–19: Cont as for round 3, working 3dc, 2ch into every ch-sp of previous round, and [3dc, 2ch, 3dc] into every corner, and changing

color following the sequence set out on page 48.
Fasten off and weave in ends.

{04} Make the edging for the back}

Starting from a corner and with yarn A, 3ch (counts as 1dc), 2dc, 2ch, 3dc to make the corner. Make the edging by working 1dc into every st, and work the corners as previously set [3dc, 2ch, 3dc], then join with sl st into third of 3ch. Fasten off and weave in ends.

{05} Finishing off

You can choose to sew the front and back of the cushion together, but here the seams were crocheted together (see page 138) to achieve a good, firm edging. Whichever method you use, join the front and back of the cushion together on three sides. On the fourth side, partially seam the side together, leaving the central third open so you can insert a cushion pad. Attach the button half way along this edge (a gap in the crochet work will serve as the buttonhole).

DESIGNED BY
ILARIA CHIARATTI

Granny square blanket with edging

{ *This blanket takes the mainstay of crochet, the traditional granny square, and overhauls it for a modern look. The granny square offered a way of using up scraps and oddments of leftover yarn, and featured random color combinations. Here the color combinations are partly fixed and partly random, and the choice of warm and bold shades makes this a vivid and eye-catching piece.*

MATERIALS

50g balls (186 yards/170 meters) of Sheepjeswol Cotton 8, four in #716 (orange) (A) and #714 (yellow) (B), five in #665 (dark aqua) (C), three in #663 (light aqua) (D) and #502 (white) (E), and two in each of #720 (bright pink) (F), #563 (cobalt blue) (G), and #642 (apple green) (H), or similar yarn (Sport, #2 fine)

Crochet hook, size B1/C2 (2.5 mm)

Tapestry needle

SIZE

About 67" × 55" (170 × 139.5 cm)

GAUGE

One granny square motif is about 5" (12.5 cm) square.

FEATURED TECHNIQUES

- Making a square from a central chain (page 108)
- Creating a crochet edge on a crochet fabric (page 130)

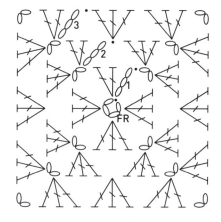

Granny square motif (rounds 1–3): make 120

BEFORE YOU BEGIN

You will need to make a total of 120 granny squares. Each square consists of six rounds. Rounds 1 and 2 are always worked in the same colors (yarn A, then yarn B). Rounds 3–5 are random (use the colors of your choice), but work rounds 4 and 5 in the same color. Round 6 is always worked in yarn C. Therefore, for every motif, the inner two rounds and the outer round are made in the same colors each time.

On rounds 3–6, on the sides of your granny square, work the 3dc groups into the sps between the 3dc groups on the previous round, and work the corners by making [3dc, 2ch, 3dc] through the 2ch-sps of the previous round.

DESIGNED BY
ANITA MUNDT

METHOD

{01} Make the granny square motifs (make 120)

Foundation ring: With yarn A, 4ch, join with sl st to form a ring.

Round 1: 3ch (counts as 1dc), 2dc, 2ch, [3dc, 2ch] three times, sl st to third of 3ch to join. Fasten off.

Round 2: With yarn B, join yarn to any corner 2ch-sp, 3ch (counts as 1dc), 2dc, 2ch, 3dc all into the same sp, [3dc, 2ch, 3dc in next corner-sp] three times, sl st to third of 3ch to join. Fasten off.

Round 3: With any of yarns D–H, join yarn to any corner 2ch-sp, 3ch (counts as 1dc), 2dc, 2ch, 3dc all into the same sp, [3dc in next sp, 3dc, 2ch, 3dc in next corner-sp] three times, 3dc in next sp, sl st to third of 3ch to join. Fasten off.

Round 4: With any color other than yarn C, join yarn to any corner 2ch-sp, 3ch (counts as 1dc), 2dc, 2ch, 3dc all into the same sp, *[3dc in next sp] twice, [3dc, 2ch, 3dc in next corner-sp], rep from * three times, [3dc in next sp] twice, sl st to third of 3ch to join. Fasten off.

Round 5: With same color yarn as round 4, sl st to next corner 2ch-sp, 3ch (counts as 1dc), 2dc, 2ch, 3dc all into the same sp, *[3dc in next sp] three times, [3dc, 2ch, 3dc in next corner-sp], rep from * three times, [3dc in next sp] three times, sl st to third of 3ch to join. Fasten off.

Round 6: With yarn C, join yarn to any corner 2ch-sp, 3ch (counts as

Crochet Story

I always loved the look of crochet, but when I asked my great-grandmother to teach me how to do it, she said I wouldn't be able to as I'm left-handed. I believed this for years and was really disappointed. Then one day I saw an internet video showing left-handed people the basic crochet stitches, and I was away!

1dc), 2dc, 2ch, 3dc all into the same sp, *[3dc in next sp] four times, [3dc, 2ch, 3dc in next corner-sp], rep from * three times, [3dc in next sp] four times, sl st to third of 3ch to join. Fasten off and weave in all ends. Block the motifs, then join the squares together to make a rectangle of 10 squares by 12.

{02} Make the border

Round 1: With yarn C, join yarn to any corner, 3ch (counts as 1dc), 2dc, 2ch, 3dc, [3dc in every sp along edge of blanket, 3dc, 2ch, 3dc in each corner] three times, 3dc in every sp along final edge of blanket. Sl st to third of initial 3ch to join.
Round 2: 1sc into every st around each edge, sl st to join to first st. Fasten off.
Round 3: With yarn D, 1hdc into every st around each edge, working 2ch in each corner. Sl st to join to first st. Fasten off.
Round 4: With yarn E, 1hdc into every st around each edge, working 2ch in each corner. Sl st to join to first st. Fasten off.
Round 5: With yarn C, 1hdc into every st around each edge, working 2ch in each corner. Sl st to join to first st. Fasten off.
Round 6: With yarn B, 3ch (counts as 1dc), 2dc, 2ch, 3dc into first corner, *[skip 3 sts, 3dc in next st, 1ch] along edge, [3dc, 2ch, 3dc] in corner, rep from * three times, [skip 3 sts, 3dc in next st, 1ch] along final edge, sl st to

join to first st. Fasten off.
Round 7: With yarn A, join yarn in corner-sp, 3ch (counts as 1dc), 2dc, 2ch, 3dc in first corner, *[3dc in each sp, 1ch] along edge, [3dc, 2ch, 3dc] in each corner, rep from * three times, [3dc in each sp, 1ch] along final edge, sl st to join to first st. Fasten off.
Round 8: With yarn F, work as for round 7.
Round 9: With yarn C, 1sc in every st, sl st to join to first st. Fasten off.
Round 10: Rejoin yarn C in any corner, *Work 1dc, 1ch, 1dc 1ch, 1dc all in the same corner st to make a corner, skip 1 st, [1dc, 2ch, skip

2 sts, 3dc in next 3 sts, 2ch, skip 2 sts] all the way along edge, rep from * three times, sl st to join to first st.
Round 11: *3ch (counts as 1dc), 2dc in same st, 1ch, picot (work picot with 3ch, join first ch to last ch with sl st), 1ch, 3dc in next st, 2ch, skip 2 sts (makes corner), sl st into top of dc from previous round, [2ch, skip 2 sts, 3dc in next st, 1ch, picot, 1ch, 3dc into next st, 2ch, skip 2 sts, sl st into top of the dc from previous round] along edges, rep from * three times, at end of final straight edge 2ch then join to first st with sl st. Fasten off and weave in all ends. Block the border.

Retro-style pot holders

These two pot holders will add a little 1950s glamour to your kitchen. The round pot holder is worked in red, aqua, and coral—a classic mid-century combination. A pretty, tweedy look was created by working with two different colored strands of yarn held together. The square pot holder features nubby popcorn stitch stripes; chunky textured pot holders are the most practical for handling hot pans.

MATERIALS

Round pot holder
50g balls (170 yards/155 meters) of DMC Natura Just Cotton, one in each of Passion (red) #23 (A), Terracotta #40 (B), Ibiza (white) #01 (C), Sable #03 (D), and Aquamarine #25 (E), or similar yarn (Sport, #2 fine)

Square pot holder
50g (170 yards/155 meters) balls of DMC Natura Just Cotton, one in each of Ibiza (white) #01 (A), Safran #47 (B), Green Smoke #54 (C), Golden Lemon #43 (D), Passion (red) #23 (E), and Gris Argent (gray) #09 (F), or similar yarn (Sport, #2 fine)

Crochet hooks, size C2 (3 mm) and G6 (4 mm)

Tapestry needle

SIZE

Round pot holder: about 8¼" (21 cm) in diameter
Square pot holder: about 8" (20.5 cm) square

GAUGE

Accurate gauge is not essential for these projects, but may alter the yarn amounts required.

DESIGNED BY EMMA LAMB

FEATURED TECHNIQUES

Round pot holder
- Working in the round (page 102)
- Increasing around the ring (page 106)
- Joining a new yarn (page 100)
- Working stitches into spaces (page 125)
- Making shells (page 128)
- Making a button loop (here used as a hanging loop) (page 142)

Square pot holder
- Working rows of double crochet (page 97)
- Making popcorn stitch (page 122)
- Making a button loop (here used as a hanging loop) (page 142)

METHOD: ROUND POT HOLDER

{01} Before you begin

The whole pot holder is made with two yarns held together. You will need to change one color several times for this project; the first time is on round 5, when you break yarn C and knot it with yarn E. Ensure that your knot is as close to your work as possible, as this will make it easier to hide when you come to weaving in your loose ends later.

{02} Make the pot holder

Base ring: Holding yarns A and B together and using a C2 hook, 5ch, sl st to form ring.

Round 1: 4ch (counts as 1dc and 1ch), [1dc, 1ch] seven times, sl st into third of 4ch. (8dc)

Round 2: Sl st into next ch-sp, 3ch (counts as 1dc), 1dc into same sp, 1ch, [2dc, 1ch] into each ch-sp to end, sl st into third of 3ch. (8 groups of 2dc)

Round 3: 3ch (counts as 1dc), [3dc, 1ch] seven times, 2dc, sl st into second of 3ch. (8 groups of 3dc)

Round 4: Sl st into next ch-sp, 3ch (counts as 1dc), 1dc, 1ch, 2dc all into same sp, [2dc, 1ch, 2dc, 1ch] into each ch-sp seven times, sl st into third of 3ch. Fasten off both yarns. (16 groups of 2dc)

Round 5: With yarns C and D, join yarn into any ch-sp of previous round, 4ch (counts as 1dc and 1ch), [3dc, 1ch] into each ch-sp fifteen times, 2dc, change yarn C to yarn E, sl st into third of 4ch. (16 groups of 3dc)

Round 6: Sl st into next ch-sp, 3ch (counts as 1dc), 1dc, 1ch, 2dc, 1ch into same sp, 1ch, [2dc, 1ch, 2dc, 1ch] into each ch-sp to end, change one color (yarn E to yarn B), sl st into third of 3ch. (32 groups of 2dc)

Round 7: 3ch (counts as 1dc), 2dc into each ch-sp 31 times, 1dc, change one color (yarn D to A), sl st into second of 3ch. (32 groups of 2dc)

Round 8: Sl st into next sp, 3ch (counts as 1dc), 1dc into same sp, 1ch, [2dc, 1ch] into each sp to end, sl st into third of 3ch. (32 groups of 2dc)

Round 9: 3ch (counts as 1dc), 3dc into each ch-sp 31 times, 2dc, sl st into second of 3ch. Fasten off both colors. (32 groups of 3dc)

Round 10: With yarns D and E, join yarn into any sp of previous round, 3ch (counts as 1dc), 3dc into each sp 31 times, 2dc, change one color (yarn E to yarn C), sl st into third of 3ch. (32 groups of 3dc)

Round 11: Sl st into next sp, 3ch (counts as 1dc), 2dc into same sp, 1ch, [3dc, 1ch] into each sp to end, sl st into third of 3ch. (32 groups of 3dc)

{03} Make the edging and the hanging loop

Round 12: 1ch, 1sc into same sp as joining sl st, 1sc into each of next 2 sts and ch-sp, 12ch (to make the hanging loop), 1sc into next ch-sp, cont the round working 1sc into each st and ch-sp, sl st into first sc.

Round 13: 1ch, work another round of sc sts with 15 sc sts into 12-ch hanging loop.
Fasten off both yarns and weave in ends.

METHOD: SQUARE POT HOLDER

{01} Before you begin

See page 122 for popcorn stitch. Note that in this design, each popcorn is made of 7dc.

See page 41 for the standing stitch method of joining a new yarn.

Work the colors for the popcorn rows as follows:

Stripes 1 and 6 = yarn B
Stripes 2 and 8 = yarn C
Stripes 3 and 7 = yarn D
Stripes 4 and 9 = yarn E
Stripe 5 = yarn F

{02} Make the pot holder

Foundation chain: With yarn A and G6 hook, 49ch, turn.

Row 1: Starting in fourth ch from hook, work a row of 47dc. Secure your working loop by passing your ball of yarn through this loop and pulling it tight. Do not cut your yarn, as you will pick it up again once you have completed your first popcorn row.

For this pot holder there is a right side and a wrong side. Place your work flat with the loose yarn to the right; the back of the row you have just worked should be facing up. This is your right side.

Row 2 (popcorn row): With RS facing, work the first popcorn row.

With yarn B and the standing stitch starting technique, [2dc, pop] fifteen times, 2dc. Fasten off yarn B.

Row 3: With RS facing, pick up yarn A and create a working loop in first dc of popcorn row, 2ch (counts as 1dc) and 1dc into same place, [skip pop st, 2dc, 1dc] to end, turn. (47 sts)

Row 4: 3ch (counts as 1dc) and work a row of 47dc. Secure your working loop as before.

Rows 2–4 set the pattern. Rep rows 2–4 seven more times, working the popcorn rows following the color sequence set in step 1.

Work row 2 (popcorn row) once more in yarn E, then work row 3 once more in yarn A before starting the edging.

{03} Make the edging

With RS facing, work the edging and hanging loop as follows:

Round 1: 1ch, *evenly work 54sc along side edge, 2ch, evenly work 47sc along next edge*, 15ch (to form hanging loop), rep from * to *, 2ch, sl st into 1st sc.

Round 2: 1ch, work a round of sc sts, with 2sc into each 2-ch corner-sp and 22sc in 15ch-sp of the hanging loop.

Fasten off yarn and weave in all loose ends.

Crochet Story

As a self-confessed color obsessive, it should be no surprise that my favorite part of any project is choosing the colors. I can ponder over combinations for hours! For these doilies and pot holders I knew I wanted a retro 1950s-style vibe but with a fresh twist on some classic color combinations, and an innovative tweed look.

Lacy stripes bolster

A pretty, lacy pattern made up of combined shell and trellis stitches worked up in boldly colored stripes are the main ingredients of this project. Circular motifs based on a variation of the perennial granny square make up the ends of the bolster cover.

MATERIALS

50g balls (145 yards/133 meters) of Annell Rapido, two in each of Light cyan #3222 (A), Orange #3221 (B), Pink #3277 (C), Light pink #3233 (D), Light gray #3356 (E), and White #3260 (F), or similar yarn (DK, #3 light)

Crochet hook, size G6 (4 mm)

Tapestry needle

Four buttons, about ¾" (2 cm) in diameter

Sewing thread and needle

Bolster cushion to fit

DESIGNED BY
ILARIA CHIARATTI

SIZE

17" (43 cm) long; 8½" (21.5 cm) in diameter

GAUGE

Accurate gauge is not essential for this project. Add more rows to fit a larger-circumference bolster.

BEFORE YOU BEGIN

The color sequence for the main part of the bolster cover is:
*2 rows in yarn A
2 rows in yarn B
3 rows in yarn C
2 rows in yarn D
2 rows in yarn E**
2 rows in yarn F*
Rep from * to * four times, then rep from * to ** once (63 rows worked in total).

The color sequence for the round bolster cover ends is:
2 rounds in yarn A
2 rounds in yarn B
2 rounds in yarn C
2 rounds in yarn D
1 round in yarn F

FEATURED TECHNIQUES

- Working trellis stitches (page 127)
- Working shells (page 128)
- Working fans (page 129)
- Creating a crochet edge on a crochet fabric (page 130)
- Crocheting seams together (page 138)

Crochet Story

When I was designing this pattern, I had in mind a solution that would leave a glimpse of the underlying color of the bolster, which had a nice bright pink cover. I decided to use bold colors that would create a nice contrast with each other, keeping the pink as the main color. The deliberately mismatched white buttons add another playful touch.

Stitch pattern for main part

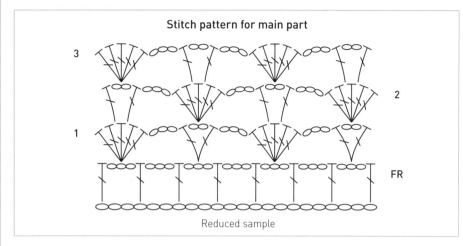

Reduced sample

METHOD

{01} Make the main part of the bolster cover

Change yarns for the color sequence as set out in Before You Begin.

Foundation row: Make 78ch (72ch for foundation row, plus 3ch counts as 1dc, plus 3ch), 1dc into ninth ch from hook, *3ch, skip 2ch, 1dc in next ch, rep from * to end of row, turn. (25dc)

Row 1: 3ch (counts as 1dc), 2ch, 1dc in same point at base of 3ch, *3ch, skip 3ch-sp, 5dc in next 3ch-sp, 3ch, skip next 3ch-sp, 1dc, 2ch, 1dc in next 3ch-sp, rep from * four times, 5dc in next 3ch-sp, 3ch, 1dc, 2ch, 1dc in final 3ch-sp, turn. (7 blocks of [1dc, 2ch, 1dc] and 6 blocks of 5dc)

Row 2: 3ch (counts as 1dc), work 4dc in same ch-sp, *3ch, skip next 3ch-sp, 1dc (worked between second and third dc of 5dc-block of previous row), 2ch, 1dc (worked between third and fourth dc of 5dc-block of previous row), 3ch, skip next 3ch-sp, 5dc in 2ch-sp (between the two dc sts), rep from * five times, turn. (7 blocks of 5dc and 6 blocks of [1dc, 2ch, 1dc])

Row 3: Sl st into first st, 1dc (worked between second and third dc of 5dc-block of previous row), 2ch, 1dc (worked between third and fourth dc of 5dc-block of previous row), *3ch, skip next 3ch-sp, 5dc in 2ch-sp (worked between the two dc sts of previous row), 3ch, skip next 3ch-sp, make 1dc (worked between second and third dc of 5dc-block of previous row), 2ch, 1dc (worked between third and fourth dc of 5dc-block of previous row), rep from * to end of row, turn. (7 blocks of [1dc, 2ch, 1dc] and 6 blocks of 5dc)

Rep rows 2 and 3 until you have 63 rows in total.

Row 64: With yarn F, *1dc between every dc of 5dc-block of the previous row (4dc), 2dc in next 3ch-sp, 2dc in 2ch-sp (worked between the two dc sts of previous row), 2dc in next 3ch-sp, rep from * five times, 1dc between every dc of 5dc-block of the previous row (4dc). (64dc) Fasten off and weave in ends.

{02} Make the side borders

Row 1: With yarn F, make an edging for both long sides of the rectangle. Starting from one corner, 3ch (counts as 1dc), 3ch, work [1dc, 3ch] evenly in each sp between each row 2 and 3, ending with 1dc in final sp, turn. (32dc)

Row 2: 3ch (counts as 1dc), 2dc in same sp, then work 3dc in every 3ch-sp of previous row, turn. (96dc)
Row 3: As row 2.
Fasten off and weave in ends.
Rep on second edge.

{03} Make the round bolster ends (make 2)
Change yarns for the color sequence as set out in Before You Begin.
Foundation ring: With yarn A, 4ch, join with sl st to form a ring.
Round 1: 3ch (counts as 1dc), 7dc into ring, join with sl st into third of 3ch. (8dc)
Round 2: 3ch (counts as 1dc), 1dc, 1ch in the same sp at base of 3ch, *2dc, 1ch in sp between next two dc, rep from * to end, join with sl st into third of 3ch. Fasten off. (8 groups of 2dc)
Round 3: Join yarn B in any sp of previous round, 3ch (counts as 1dc), 2dc, 2ch in the same sp at base of 3ch, *3dc, 2ch in next ch-sp, rep from * to end, join with sl st into third of 3ch. (8 groups of 3dc)
Round 4: 3ch (counts as 1dc), 1dc, 1ch, 2dc, 1ch in same sp at base of 3ch, *[2dc, 1ch] twice in next 2ch-sp, rep from * to end, join with sl st into third of 3ch. Fasten off. (16 groups of 2dc)
Round 5: Join yarn C in any sp of previous round, 3ch (counts as 1dc), 1dc, 2ch in same sp at base of 3ch, *2dc, 2ch in next ch-sp, rep from * to end, join with sl st into third of 3ch. (16 groups of 2dc)

Round 6: 3ch (counts as 1dc), 1dc, 1ch, 2dc, 1ch in same sp at base of 3ch, *[2dc, 1ch, 2dc, 1ch] in next 2ch-sp, rep from * to end, join with sl st into third of 3ch. Fasten off. (32 groups of 2dc)
Round 7: Join yarn D in any sp of previous round, 3ch (counts as 1dc), 1dc, 1ch in same sp at base of 3ch, *2dc, 1ch in next ch-sp, rep from * to end, join with sl st into third of 3ch (32 groups of 2dc)
Round 8: Work as for round 7 but cont with yarn D. Fasten off.
Round 9: Join yarn F in any sp of previous round, 3ch (counts as 1dc), 2dc in same sp at base of 3ch, *3dc in next ch-sp, rep from * to end, join with sl st into third of 3ch. (32 groups of 3dc)
Fasten off and weave in ends.

{04} Make up the bolster cover
Now that you have the three parts ready (the rectangle and the two circles), secure them on the cushion using a few pins. With yarn F, sew all the parts together, leaving an opening to insert the cushion pad. Sew four buttons on the white edge of the main bolster part. The spaces in the lacy stitch pattern will form the buttonholes.

Hexagon motif blanket

Making motifs is a satisfying way to create modular items such as blankets and throws. You can make as many motifs as you like, so it's easy to custom-make a piece to the size you want. Motifs also offer an exciting way to experiment with color; here vibrant colors were used in random combinations, linked with a cream background.

MATERIALS

50g balls (186 yards/170 meters) of Sheepjeswol Cotton 8; five of balls Ecru #501 (ecru) (MC), two in each of #663 (light aqua), #665 (dark aqua), #510 (red), #717 (dark red), and one in each of #517 (light green), #669 (moss green), #714 (yellow), and #639 (orange), or similar yarn (Sport, #2 fine)

Crochet hook, size B1/C2 (2.5 mm)

Tapestry needle

SIZE

About 47¼" (120 cm) square

GAUGE

Each motif measures about 3½" (9 cm) across at the widest points.

FEATURED TECHNIQUES

- Measuring the gauge of a motif (page 11)
- The magic loop method of starting a round (page 104)
- Making clusters (page 120)
- Joining motifs together (pages 139 and 140)

Hexagon motifs:
Work rounds 1–3 for both circle center and starburst center motifs. Work rounds 4–5 as shown above for the circle center motifs; see page 66 for written instructions for round 4 of the starburst center motifs.

DESIGNED BY ANITA MUNDT

BEFORE YOU BEGIN

You will make 196 full hexagons and 14 half hexagons. Of the 196 full hexagons, about a quarter should feature a starburst center and the remaining three-quarters a circle center. (This does not need to be an exact ratio, as long as the total number is 196.)

Rounds 1–3 are each made in a different color, in a random sequence; the motif is always completed in cream yarn.

Round 2 of each motif features a 2dc-cluster. Work this as follows:

Yarn over (yo), push hook through stitch, pick up yarn and pull through so there are three loops on your hook, yo and pull through first two loops, leaving two loops on your hook. Yo and push through same stitch, pick up yarn and pull through, so there are four loops on the hook. Yo and pull through first two loops, leaving three loops on the hook. Yo and pull through all three remaining loops.

The motifs are joined by placing two with RS together, sl st through corner-sps, 3ch, then sl st through both motifs in between each set of 3dc. Cont like this along one side of the motif, ending with sl st in final corner-sp. For more on joining motifs, see pages 139–140.

METHOD

{01} Make the circle center motifs
Make a magic loop, then work as follows:
Round 1: 3ch (counts as 1dc), 11dc into the circle, sl st into third of 3ch to join round. Fasten off. (12dc)
Round 2: Join new color through any st on previous round, work 3ch (counts as 1dc) and 1dc into same st, 1ch, [2dc-cluster, 1ch into dc on previous round] eleven times, sl st into third of 3ch to join round. Fasten off. (12 2dc-clusters)
Round 3: Join new color through any ch-sp on previous round, work 3ch (counts as 1dc) and 2dc in same sp (to make 3dc group), [3dc in next ch-sp] eleven times (each 3dc creates a "set" that sits together with a space in between), sl st into third of 3ch to join round. Fasten off. (12 3dc groups)
Round 4: Join MC in any gap between sets of 3dc on previous

Circle center motif.

Starburst center motif.

round, [3ch, sc into gap between next set of 3dc] twelve times, join round with sl st.
Round 5: Work 3ch (counts as 1dc), 2dc, 2ch, 3dc in 3ch-sp, [3dc in next 3ch-sp, 3dc, 2ch, 3dc in next 3ch-sp] five times, 3dc in next 3ch-sp, sl st into third of 3ch to join round. Fasten off and weave in ends.

{02} Make the starburst center motifs
Make a magic loop, then work rounds 1–3 as for circle center motifs.
Round 4: Join MC to any gap between sets of 3dc on previous round, work 3ch (counts as 1dc), 2dc, 2ch, 3dc into same gap, [3dc into gap between next two sets of 3dc, 3dc, 2ch, 3dc in next gap

Half hexagon motif.

st at same end where you began previous round.

Row 4: Sl st into top of first dc, 1ch, 1sc into gap between first two sets of 3dc, [3ch, 1sc into gap between next set of 3dc] five times, 1ch, sl st into top of final dc, turn.

Row 5: Work 3ch (counts as 1dc) and 1dc into ch-sp, [3dc into next 3ch-sp] twice, [3dc, 2ch, 3dc into next 3ch-sp, 3dc into next 3ch-sp] twice, 2dc into top of ch-sp on previous row, sl st and fasten off. Weave in all ends.

{04} Making up the blanket

Block each hexagon motif, then join motifs together in rows of 14. Join the rows together in 14 lines to make a blanket consisting of 14 x 14 hexagon motifs (196 in all). Fill the spaces on the side edges with half hexagon motifs to make the side edges straight.

{05} Make the border

With MC, make 1hdc in each st down both the straight edges only. Fasten off yarn and weave in ends.

between two sets of 3dc] five times, 3dc into gap between next two sets of 3dc, sl st into third of 3ch to join round. Fasten off and weave in ends.

{03} Make the half hexagon motifs (make 14)

Make a magic loop, then work as follows:

Row 1: 3ch (counts as 1dc), 6dc, sl st, fasten off yarn. Join new yarn with sl st at same end where you began previous round.

Row 2: Work 3ch (counts as 1dc), 1dc into same st, 1ch, [2dc-cluster, 1ch into dc on previous row] six times, sl st, fasten off yarn. Join new yarn with sl st at same end where you began previous round.

Row 3: 3ch (counts as 1dc) into top of first 2dc-cluster, [3dc into ch-sp on previous round] six times, 1dc into top of final 2dc-cluster, sl st, fasten off yarn. Join MC with sl

Crochet Story

My plain cream sofa needed a little something to pull together all the colors from the rest of the room. I'm not a fan of cushions, so decided to make a blanket to throw over the back of the sofa. I needed to include quite a few colors, but as they are contained to only the centers of the hexagons, the finished blanket doesn't look too busy.

Monster gadget covers

{ *These gadget covers are easy to make—the basic shape is just a rectangle of single crochet rows. The iPad and Kindle covers close with a flap, made by extending the back and folding it over the top, with decreases at the sides to make an envelope shape. The iPod cover is open at one end, with a flap that fastens on the back.* }

MATERIALS

50g balls (170 yards/155 meters) of Sirdar Country Style, two in Soft Teal #602 (A) and one in each of Honey #399 (B), Amber #394 (D), Apples #599 (E), White #412 (F), Heather #529 (G), and Rustic Red #396 (H), or similar yarn (DK, #3 light)

Small amount of black DK-weight yarn (C)

Crochet hook, size E4 (3.5 mm)

One green and one red button, each about ¾" (2 cm) in diameter

Velcro fastening

Small black beads for the centers of eyes (optional if you prefer not to work French knots)

SIZE

Measurements for the finished items are for the main case, without extra horns, feet etc.

iPad cover: 8" × 10" (20.5 × 25.5 cm)

Kindle cover:
Small: 5½" × 7½" (14 × 19 cm)—to fit Kindle up to 4¾" × 6¾" (12 × 17 cm)
Medium: 5¾" × 8¼" (14.5 × 21 cm)—to fit Kindle up to 5" × 7½" (12.5 × 19 cm)
Large: 6¼" × 8¼" (16 × 21 cm)—to fit Kindle up to 5½" × 7½" (14 × 19 cm)

iPod cover: 3½" × 5½" (9 × 14 cm) (will fit all iPod touches, and iPhone)

GAUGE

18.5 sts and 24 rows to 4" (10 cm) square with E4 hook over single crochet.

After working a few rows of the main part of each case, it is worth checking your gauge to make sure that the case will end up the size stated.

FEATURED TECHNIQUES

- Working rows of single crochet (page 93)
- Making bobbles (page 123)
- Making button loops and buttonholes (pages 141 and 142)
- Surface embroidery (page 134)
- Surface crochet (page 135)

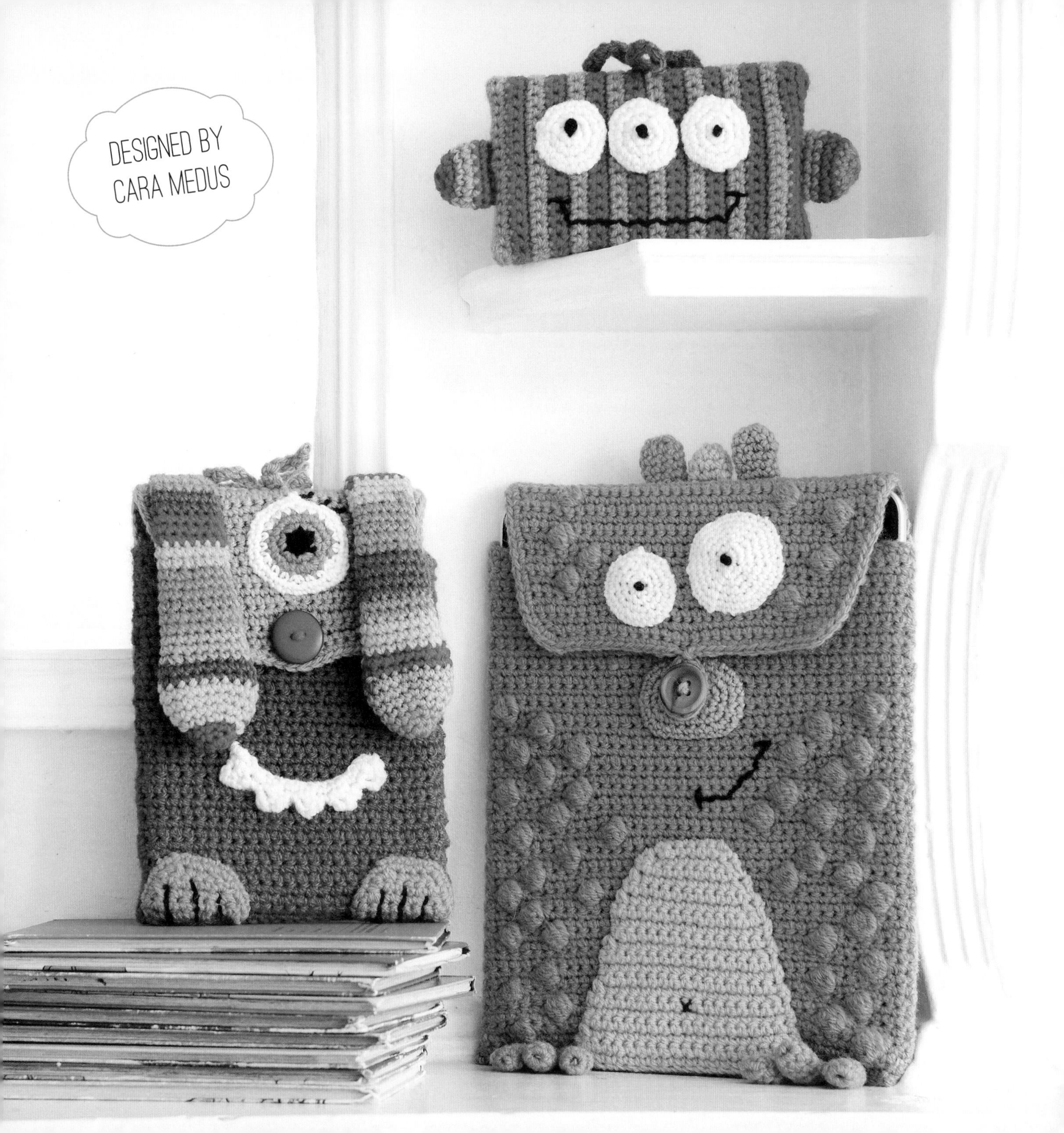
DESIGNED BY
CARA MEDUS

BEFORE YOU BEGIN

To work a sc2tog decrease: work two single crochet stitches together over the next two stitches (decrease by one stitch).

The iPad cover features bobble stitches (see page 123).

MB (Make Bobble) as follows:
*Yarn over (yo) and insert hook into next st, yo and draw yarn through st, yo and draw yarn through first two loops on hook, rep from * four times, yo and draw through all six loops on hook.

The pieces that specify "leaving a long tail of yarn" after fastening off are those that need the extra length of yarn for sewing to the main case.

Crochet Story

When I made the main piece of the iPad cover, the gauge varied as I went along, so I tried blocking it into the shape I wanted. I was relieved that it worked, so take it from me, there is hope if you have similar problems! My son took a shine to these monsters and christened them Chomper, Nibbles and Tryclops. Looks like I may be making one for his birthday ...

METHOD: IPAD COVER

{01} Make the front
With yarn A, ch39.
Row 1 (RS): 1ch, 1sc in each ch beg with second ch from hook, turn. (38 sts)
Row 2: 1ch, 1sc in each st to end, turn.
Rep last row twice.

Start making the bobbles on the front:
Row 5 (RS): 1ch, 3sc, MB, 1sc in each st to last 5 sts, MB, 4sc, turn.
Row 6 and every WS row: 1ch, 1sc in each st to end, turn.
Row 7: 1ch, 6sc, MB, 1sc in each st to last 8 sts, MB, 7sc, turn.
Row 9: 1ch, 4sc, MB, 1sc in each st to last 4 sts, MB, 3sc, turn.
Row 11: 1ch, 7sc, MB, 1sc in each st to last 7 sts, MB, 6sc, turn.
Row 13: 1ch, 3sc, MB, 1sc in each st to end, turn.
Row 15: 1ch, 7sc, MB, 1sc in each st to last 8 sts, MB, 3sc, MB, 3sc, turn.
Row 17: 1ch, 4sc, MB, 1sc in each st to last 6 sts, MB, 5sc, turn.
Row 19: 1ch, 3sc, MB, 1sc in each st to last 11 sts, MB, 6sc, MB, 3sc, turn.
Row 21: 1ch, 5sc, MB, 4sc, MB, 1sc in each st to last 6 sts, MB, 5sc, turn.
Row 23: 1ch, 8sc, MB, 1sc in each st to last 9 sts, MB, 8sc, turn.
Row 25: 1ch, 4sc, MB, 1sc in each st to last 13 sts, MB, 7sc, MB, 4sc, turn.
Row 27: 1ch, 7sc, MB, 4sc, MB, 1sc in each st to last 8 sts, MB, 7sc, turn.
Row 29: 1ch, 3sc, MB, 6sc, MB, 1sc in each st to last 10 sts, MB, 5sc, MB, 3sc, turn.
Row 31: 1ch, 6sc, MB, 11sc in each st to last 7 sts, MB, 6sc, turn.
Row 33: 1ch, [4sc, MB] twice, 1sc in each st to last 10 sts, [MB, 4sc] twice, turn.
Row 35: 1ch, 7sc, MB, 1sc in each st to last 7 sts, MB, 6sc, turn.
Row 37: 1ch, 3sc, MB, 1sc in each st to last 4 sts, MB, 3sc, turn.
Cont working rows of plain sc (as row 2) until the front measures 9" (23 cm).
Fasten off and weave in ends.

{02} Make the back
With yarn A, 39ch.
Row 1 (RS): 1ch, 1sc in each ch beg with second ch from hook, turn. (38 sts)
Row 2: 1ch, 1sc in each st to end, turn.
Rep last row until back measures the same as front (9"/23 cm), ending with a WS row.
Next row (RS): Sl st, 1sc in each st to last st, leave last st unworked and turn. (36 sts)
Rep last row until back measures 10" (25 cm), ending with WS row.
Next row (RS): 1ch, and working in **back loops only** of the sts of the previous row, 1sc in each st to end, turn. This creates a fold line.

Make the flap:
Next row (WS): 1ch, (working in

both loops as normal) 1sc in each st to end, turn.
Rep last row twice.

Start decreasing and make the bobbles for the flap:
Row 1 (RS): 1ch, sc2tog, 3sc, MB, 1sc in each st to last 10 sts, MB, 7sc, sc2tog, turn. (34 sts)
Row 2 and every WS row: 1ch, sc in each st to end, turn.
Row 3: 1ch, 1sc in each st to last 4 sts, MB, 3sc.
Row 5: 1ch, sc2tog, 2sc, MB, 1sc in each st to last 2 sts, sc2tog, turn. (32 sts)
Row 7: 1ch, 6sc, MB, 1sc in each st to last 4 sts, MB, 3sc, turn.
Row 9: 1ch, sc2tog, 2sc, MB, 1sc in each st to last 2 sts, sc2tog, turn. (30 sts)
Row 11: 1ch, 1sc in each st to last 6 sts, MB, 5sc, turn.
Row 13: 1ch, sc2tog, 1sc in each st to last 2 sts, sc2tog, turn. (28 sts)
Row 14 (WS): As row 13. (26 sts)
Fasten off and weave in ends.

With WS facing, match the front and the back and oversew the side and bottom seams.

Make the flap edging and the button loop as follows.
Begin the edging for the flap at the point on the back where the seam ends. Rejoin yarn A with RS facing. Work sc evenly up to the fold line

and down the side of the flap with 1sc in every row end and 2sc in the corner st.

When working along the lower edge of the flap, make 13sc to center and work the button loop as follows:

8ch and sl st back into the sc at the base of the ch, turn.
1ch and 12sc into the loop, sl st back into the sc at the base of the loop, turn.
Carry on working sc into each st around the rest of the flap until you

reach the seam at the back.
Fasten off and weave in ends.

{03} Make the tummy

With yarn B, make 21ch.
Row 1 (RS): 1ch, 1sc in each st to end, turn. (20 sts)
Row 2: 1ch, 1sc in each st to end, turn.
Row 3: 1ch, sc2tog, 1sc in each st to last 2 sts, sc2tog, turn. (18 sts)
Cont in plain sc until 20 rows have been worked, with a decreasing row as set in row 3 on rows 7, 11, 15, 17, 19 and 20.
Fasten off, leaving a long tail of yarn. Weave in the starting end. With yarn C, sew a small cross in the center of the sixth row. Sew the tummy to the front, lining up the bottom edge with the bottom seam and placing it centrally on the front.

{04} Make the horns

With yarn D, make 2ch. Work 8sc in the first of these ch and cont working on these 8 sts with a sc in each st. Work in a spiral without closing off the round with a sl st until the horn measures 1¼" (3 cm) long.
Fasten off, leaving a long tail of yarn. Rep with yarn B, making a horn ¾" (2 cm) long, and with yarn E, making a horn 1" (2.5 cm). Sew the three horns in the center along the fold line at the top.

{05} Make the toes (make 6)

With yarn D, make 2ch. Work 6sc in the first of these ch and cont working on these 6 sts in the same fashion as the horns until each measures 1¼" (3 cm) long.
Fasten off, leaving a long tail of yarn. Sew the toes in two groups of three to the bottom seam, with each group starting about ½" (1.5 cm) away from the side seam.

{06} Make the nose

With yarn E, make 5ch.
Round 1: 3sc beg in second ch from hook, 4sc in last ch. Rotate the work 180 degrees to work along the other side of the foundation chain. Skip the ch at the base of the st just worked, 2sc, 3sc in next st, sl st to first st of round to join. (12 sts)
Round 2: 1ch, starting with st at the base of the ch, *4sc, [2sc in next st] twice, rep from * once, sl st to first ch of round to join. (16 sts)
Round 3: 1ch, *5sc, 2sc in next st, 1sc, 2sc in next st, rep from * once, sl st to first ch of round to join. (20 sts)
Round 4: 1ch, *5sc, [2sc in next st, 1sc] twice, 2sc in next st, rep from * once, sl st to first ch of round to join. (26 sts)
Fasten off, leaving a long tail of yarn. Sew the nose to the front so that the button loop will be in the right position for the button to be sewn to the center of the nose. Sew on the green button.

{07} Make the eyes

Make the large eye:
With yarn F, make a magic loop (see page 104).
Round 1: 1ch, 6sc into the loop, sl st to first ch to join. Pull the loop closed. (6 sts)
Round 2: 1ch, 2sc into each st, sl st to first ch to join. (12 sts)
Round 3: 1ch, *1sc, 2sc in next st, rep from * five times, sl st to first ch to join. (18 sts)
Round 4: 1ch, *2sc, 2sc in next st, rep from * five times, sl st to first ch to join. (24 sts)
Round 5: 1ch, *3sc, 2sc in next st, rep from * five times, sl st to first ch to join. (30 sts)
Round 6: 1ch, *4sc, 2sc in next st, rep from * five times, sl st to first ch to join. (36 sts)
Fasten off, making sure to leave a long tail of yarn.

Make the small eye:
Work as for large eye to the end of round 4.
Fasten off, leaving a long tail of yarn.

With yarn C, sew a French knot (see page 135) in the center of each eye, or use small black beads if preferred. Sew the eyes in position on the flap.

{08} Make the mouth

With yarn C, backstitch a mouth using the photograph on page 71 as a guide.

METHOD: IPOD COVER

{01} Make the cover

With yarn D, 34ch.

Row 1 (RS): 1ch, sc in each ch beg with second ch from hook, turn. (33 sts)

Row 2: 1ch, 1sc in each st to end, turn. Change to yarn H, but do not fasten off D.

Work 2 rows of plain sc.

Cont alternating two rows of D with two rows of H until work measures 5½" (14 cm), finishing with an even number of rows so that there is a completed stripe. Fasten off and weave in ends.

Fold in half so that the piece is 5½" (14 cm) long with WS facing. Backstitch a seam along the long side, taking a one-stitch seam allowance. Turn RS out and oversew the short edge seam.

{02} Make the ears

There are three stripes of color on each ear; decide which stripe of color on the main case will lay next to the ear, then start and end the ear with the alternate color, so that the stripe pattern is continued. For example, if the end stripe on the main case is in D, then start the ear with H, so that you have H/D/H and the ear will lay next to the D stripe.

Make the first ear—to be sewn on the edge with the closed seam. With H (D), make a magic loop.

Round 1: 1ch and work 6sc into the loop. Cont working on these 6 sts with 1sc in each st. Work in a spiral without closing off round with a sl st.

Round 2: 2sc in each st. Pull the magic loop closed. (12 sts)

Change to D (H) and work another two rounds of sc on these 12 sts. Change to the alternate color and rep the last two rounds once. Fasten off, leaving a long tail of yarn.

Make the second ear with flap – to be sewn on the open edge.

Rep these six rounds for the second ear, but do not fasten off at the end. Change to the alternate color, 6dc, turn. (6 sts)

Next row: 1ch, 6sc, turn.

Rep the last row four times, or until these rows of 6 sts measure about 1¼" (3 cm).

Fasten off and weave in ends.

Sew the second ear with the extra "flap" to the front open edge of the case, sewing the bottom of the ear together as you do so. Leave the flap free so it can be fastened on the back of the case with Velcro. Sew the Velcro in place to fasten the flap. Sew the first ear on the end with the closed seam, sewing the bottom of the ear together as you do so.

{03} Make the eyes (make 3)

With yarn F, work rounds 1–3 as for the large eye on the iPad cover. Fasten off, leaving a long tail of yarn. With yarn C, sew a French knot (see page 135) in the center, or use a small black bead if preferred. Sew the three eyes on to the front of the case.

{04} Make the hair

With yarn G, work as for the hair on the Kindle cover (overleaf). Fasten off, leaving a long tail of yarn and weave in the starting end. Sew to the center top of the main case.

{05} Make the mouth

With yarn C, backstitch a mouth as shown in the photograph below.

METHOD: KINDLE COVER

{01} Make the front, back and flap
The instructions are for three sizes:
Small(Medium:Large).

With yarn G, make 27(29:31)ch.
Row 1 (RS): 1ch, 1sc in each ch beg
with second ch from hook, turn.
(26:28:30 sts)
Row 2: 1ch, 1sc in each st to
end, turn.

Rep last row until work measures
6¾"(7½":7½") (17:19:19 cm), ending
with a WS row.
Next row (RS): 1ch, and working in
back loops only of the sts of the
previous row, sc in each st to end,
turn. This creates a fold line.

Make the back:
Next row (WS): 1ch, (working in both
loops as normal) 1sc in each st to
end, turn.
Rep last row until back measures
the same as front (6¾":7½":7½")
(17:19:19 cm) when folded along fold
line.
Next row (RS): Join yarn E into the
second st of the row, work 1sc in
each st to the last st, which is left
unworked, turn. (24:26:28 sts)
Cont working in rows of plain sc
on these sts for another ¾" (2 cm),
ending with a WS row.
Next row (RS): 1ch, and working in
back loops only of the sts of the
previous row, 1sc in each st to end,
turn. This creates a fold line.

Make the flap:
Next row (WS): 1ch, (working in both
loops as normal) 1sc in each st to
end, turn.
Rep last row twice.
Next row (RS): 1ch, sc2tog, 1sc in
each st to last 2 sts, sc2tog, turn.
(22:24:26 sts)
Work three rows of plain sc (as first
row of flap).
Rep last four rows twice. (18:20:22 sts)

Make the buttonhole:
Next row (RS): 1ch, sc2tog, 1sc in each
st until central 4 sts, 4ch, skip 4 sts,
1sc in each st until last 2 sts, sc2tog.
(16:18:20 sts)
Next row: 1ch, sc2tog, 1sc in each
st to 4ch-sp, 4sc in the 4ch-sp,
1sc in each st to last 2 sts, sc2tog.
(14:16:18 sts)

Fasten off and weave in ends.
Finish as for edging on the iPad cover (page 71), omitting the button loop. Sew the red button to the center front to correspond with the buttonhole. If the buttonhole is too large for the button, sew a couple of stitches at each end of the buttonhole.

{02} Make the feet (make 2)
With yarn D, 9ch.
Row 1 (RS): 1ch, 1sc in each st to end, turn. (8 sts)
Row 2: 1ch, 1sc in each st to end, turn.
Row 3: 1ch, sc2tog, 1sc in each st to last 2 sts, sc2tog, turn. (6 sts)
Row 4: As row 2.
Row 5: As row 3. (4 sts)
Leaving the yarn attached, sc evenly all the way around the outside of the foot, with 1sc in each row end and 2sc in each bottom corner. Sl st to first sc of the round to join.
Fasten off, leaving a long tail of yarn, and weave in starting end.
With yarn C, backstitch three straight lines on each foot.
Sew the feet to either side of the front, lining up the bottom edge with the fold line at the base of the front.

{03} Make the eye
Work the rounds indicated as for the large eye on the iPad cover (page 72), changing colors as follows. When changing color, work the last sl st of the round with the new color for the next round: With yarn C, make a magic loop and work round 1.

Work rounds 2 and 3 with yarn D.
Work rounds 4 and 5 with yarn F.
Fasten off, leaving a long tail of yarn and weave in starting end.
Sew the eye to the center of the flap. With yarn C, backstitch three eyelashes above the eye.

{04} Make the ears
Make 2, but for the second use the color shown in brackets.
With yarn H (D), make a magic loop.
Round 1: 1ch and work 6sc into the loop. Cont working on these 6 sts with a sc in each st. Work in a spiral without closing off the round with a sl st.
Round 2: [2sc in next st, 2sc] twice. Pull the magic loop closed. (8 sts)
Round 3: [2sc in next st, 3sc] twice. (10 sts)
Change to B (E).
Round 4: [2sc in next st, 1sc] three times, 2sc in next st, 3sc. (14 sts)
Round 5: [2sc in next st, 2sc, 2sc in next st, 3sc] twice. (18 sts)
Rounds 6 and 7: 18sc.
Change to G (H).
Rounds 8 and 9: 18sc.
Change to B (E).
Round 10: [Sc2tog, 7sc] twice. (16 sts)
Rounds 11 and 12: 16sc.
Change to D (A).
Rounds 13 and 14: 16sc.
Change to A (G).
Rounds 15, 16 and 17: 16sc.
Round 18: [Sc2tog, 6sc] twice. (14 sts)
Change to B (D).
Rounds 19 and 20: 14sc.
Change to H (A).

Rounds 21, 22 and 23: 14sc.
Change to G (B).
Rounds 24 and 25: 14sc.
Change to D (H).
Round 26: 14sc.
Round 27: [Sc2tog, 5sc] twice. (12 sts)
Round 28: 12sc.
Fasten off, leaving a long tail of yarn. Flatten the ears so that most of the color joins are at the back. Sew to the fold line on either side of the top of the flap. Sew the ends of the ears closed at the same time as joining them to the flap. Sew a few stitches on the underside of each ear to join them to the bottom of the flap.

{05} Make the teeth
With yarn F, 16ch.
Beg in second ch from hook, *3sc, turn. (3 sts for first tooth)
1ch, sc2tog, 1sc, turn. (2 sts)
1ch, sc2tog, 2 sl st down the side of the tooth.
Rep from * four times.
Fasten off, leaving a long tail of yarn and weave in starting end.
Sew in a semicircle to the front.

{06} Make the hair
With yarn A, *9ch, 8sc beg in second ch from hook, rep from *, sl st into the end of the first row of sc. Rep from * once more, and sl st into the same place as previously.
Fasten off, leaving a long tail of yarn and weave in starting end.
Sew to the fold line in the center of the flap.

Multicolored chevron throw

{ You might find it difficult to know when to stop with this chevron throw—you will always want to make one more row! This is a simple but striking pattern that will enliven your décor. The color sequence and the width of the chevrons are random, so you can play around with the design and get creative.

MATERIALS

50g balls (145 yards/133 meters) of Annell Rapido, or similar yarn (DK, #3 light); you will need five or six balls in each of the following colors (the color sequence is random, so the amounts will vary): Pink #3277, Light cyan #3222, Light green #3223, White #3260, Indigo #3224, Light gray #3356, Red #3212, and Light pink 3233

Size 3.5mm (US E4) crochet hook

Tapestry needle

SIZE

41" × 58¼" (104 × 148 cm)

GAUGE

18dc and 11 rows worked over chevron pattern to 4" (10 cm) square using E4 crochet hook. One complete chevron is about 7" (18 cm) wide.

FEATURED TECHNIQUES

- Making chevrons (pages 116–117)
- Increasing and decreasing within a row (pages 112 and 113)
- Joining a new yarn (page 100)
- Working into spaces created by stitches (page 125)
- Creating a crochet edge on a crochet fabric (page 130)

Crochet Story

When my husband and I moved to a new house, I immediately decided to make a new throw to liven up the living room. I was looking for something that was simple to make and was playful, and that would display all the colors that I like the most. The chevron pattern was ideal and the finished throw is just what I wanted!

DESIGNED BY
ILARIA CHIARATTI

BEFORE YOU BEGIN

The chevron pattern is created by working teamed pairs of increases and decreases to make waves in the crochet fabric. You will increase by working [1dc, 2ch and 1dc] all into the same space (increase by one stitch); you will decrease by working dc2tog over three stitches (work the first "leg", or partial double, into 1ch, skip 1ch, then work the second "leg" into the next ch and complete the dc2tog; decrease by one stitch). See pages 112 and 113 for more on increases and decreases.

One complete chevron is made up of 30dc. The throw is made up of six chevrons (180dc) in total: five complete chevrons are framed by a half chevron at each edge. The pattern can easily be adapted if you want to make the throw narrower or wider; simply add or subtract multiples of 30 to or from the foundation chain.

The color changes are random; you can also make the strips of color as deep as you like.

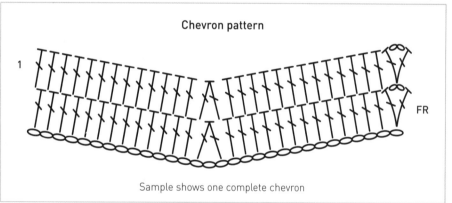

Chevron pattern

1

FR

Sample shows one complete chevron

METHOD

{01} Make the throw
Foundation row: Make 180ch (177ch plus 3ch counts as 1dc), 1dc into fourth ch from hook, 1dc into each of next 12ch, *[1dc, 2ch, 1dc] into next ch, 1dc into each of next 13ch, [dc2tog over next 3ch], 1dc into each of next 13ch, rep from * four times, [1dc, 2ch, 1dc] into next ch, 1dc into each of final 14ch, turn. (180dc)
Row 1: 3ch (counts as 1dc), 13dc (placing sts between the doubles made on the previous row), *[1dc, 2ch, 1c] into 2ch-sp, 13dc (again placing sts between doubles on previous row), [dc2tog, placing each "leg" on either side of tent shape formed by dc2tog on previous row], 13dc (placing sts between doubles on previous row), rep from * four times, [1dc, 2ch, 1dc] into next 2ch-sp, work final 14dc (placing sts between doubles on previous row), turn.
Rep row 1 until the throw is 57½" (146 cm) long.
Fasten off yarn and weave in ends.

{02} Make the edging
Here the border was worked in white yarn, but choose whatever color you feel works best.
Round 1: Joining the yarn to any corner, work the corner as follows: 3ch (counts as 1dc), 1dc, 3ch, 2dc (for the three subsequent corners, work [2dc, 3ch, 2dc]).
On the short edges of the throw at top and bottom, work 1dc between

every double on the previous row. On the long edges of the throw, place the sts between the 1dc or 3ch and the next st in the row; work 1dc and 2dc alternately into these spaces to create an even edge. Join with sl st into third of 3ch.

Round 2: Work the first corner as 3ch (counts as 1dc), 1dc, 3ch, 2dc (for the three subsequent corners, work [2dc, 3ch, 2dc]).

On the short edges of the throw, make arches: *4ch, skip 3dc, 1sc between the third and fourth doubles of previous round, rep from * until you reach the corner.

On the long edges of the throw, work 1dc between every dc on the previous round. Join with sl st into third of 3ch.

Fasten off yarn and weave in ends.

New to crochet?

This section of the book contains all the step-by-step guidance you need to get started. So grab your hook, choose your yarn, and read on—give it a couple of hours and you'll be hooked like the rest of us!

Seasoned pro?

If you've already completed a few crochet projects, use this section to build up your skill base. Jam-packed with hints, tips and techniques, you'll soon be tackling more than just granny squares. Have a go at chevrons, stripes, 3D shapes, and edgings, then try your hand at clusters, puffs, popcorns, and bobbles!

Techniques

Hooks and yarns

{ *Crochet requires relatively little equipment to get started, and because, most of the time you need only a crochet hook and a ball or yarn, it is an extremely portable craft.* }

HOOKS

Crochet hooks come in many shapes and sizes; some have thick handles, and others are very fine. Some are made from metal, others from plastic or bamboo. The hook should be comfortable to hold and should not slip in your hand while you are working your stitches.

HOOK SIZES

Hooks come in a range of sizes from small to large to suit different weights of yarn. In this book the hook sizes are given in both U.S. (alphabetical and number reference) and metric (in millimeters): for example C2 (2.75 mm). Unfortunately, there are not always equivalent sizes in both systems. When working from patterns, if you cannot obtain the size of hook suggested, use the closest size available, and always make a gauge (tension) swatch (see page 10) before you start a project in case you need to size up or down.

U.S.	Metric
–	2 mm
B1	2.25 mm
–	2.5 mm
C2	2.75 mm
–	3 mm
D3	3.25 mm

U.S.	Metric
E4	3.5 mm
F5	3.75 mm
G6	4 mm
7	4.5 mm
H8	5 mm
I9	5.5 mm

U.S.	Metric
J10	6 mm
K10½	6.5 mm
–	7 mm
L11	8 mm
M/N 13	9 mm
N/P 15	10 mm

OTHER EQUIPMENT

Apart from crochet hooks, there are one or two other pieces of equipment that you will also find useful. You don't necessarily have to buy all of it at once—and if you also knit you may find you have some items already.

SMALL SHARP SCISSORS
You will only need a small pair of sharp needlework scissors, and keep these exclusively for cutting yarn. If you keep scissors in your project bag, buy a pair with a case.

YARN CUTTER
A yarn cutter contains a sharp metal blade, encased within an ornamental casing, that can be used to slice through a yarn. Yarn cutters are often decorative and can be worn as a pendant, and are useful when traveling.

STITCH MARKERS
Usually stitch markers are made of plastic and are brightly colored so you can spot them easily. They can be used to mark the beginning/end of rounds or to mark the position of stitch detailing such as increases and decreases. You can also use scraps of waste yarn for this purpose.

PINS
The best pins for use on a crochet fabric are long, with brightly colored tips so you can see them against the yarn.

TAPE MEASURE
A tape measure is essential for checking gauge and for working to specific measurements in a pattern. A retractable dressmaker's tape measure is best: it should be strong and flexible but must not stretch.

ROW COUNTER
These are handy when working complicated designs and if you struggle to recognize rows on your crochet fabric.

TAPESTRY NEEDLE
When dealing with yarn ends or sewing crochet pieces together, it is best to use a large, blunt sewing needle. These are often referred to as knitters' sewing needles, yarn needles or tapestry needles. It is possible to get cranked sewing needles that have a slight dip toward the point end. These are very useful for sewing up because they make it easier to find the gaps between stitches.

NOTEBOOK OR SCRAPBOOK
It is a good idea to jot down any changes made to an existing pattern for future reference. Small scrapbooks are handy for holding design ideas jotted down in hurry, or cuttings from magazines to provide inspiration for future projects.

HOOK ROLL AND PROJECT BAG
It is a good idea to keep your hooks safe by storing them in specially made tool wraps or making your own. Keep all the materials and equipment you need for a work-in-progress project in a project bag, so that your crochet is always handy and portable.

YARN

It is important that you take plenty of time to choose the correct yarn (and subsequently, hook) for your project. Yarns come in many different types and are available in an extraordinary array of weights, colors, textures and fiber contents.

YARN WEIGHT

Yarns come in a variety of thicknesses, with sometimes bewildering names. Each yarn type generally works up to a certain gauge range. A good rule of thumb is the thicker the yarn, the thicker the hook. The chart below shows standard yarn weights, hook sizes, and gauge when using that hook.

TRADITIONAL CROCHET THREAD

As long as you match the hook size to the weight of yarn you have chosen, you can crochet with pretty much any weight of yarn, regardless of the market for which the yarn was intended. Many knitting yarns work extremely well when crocheted, as do rug yarns and even unconventional materials, such as string and metal wire.

Traditionally, however, crochet yarn has had a tendency to be on the fine side, often made from premium cotton or linen, to produce small, intricate stitches comparable to a lace-weight fabric. Traditional crochet cotton is still available today; it is wound onto a cardboard tube and comes in small balls weighing either 50g or 20g, depending upon the thickness of the thread. The yarns are categorized using a number system rather than an indication of ply, with numbers ranging from 5 through to 100. The higher the number on the yarn, the finer it will be—and thus the smaller the required hook.

Thread Count	Hook Size
No 5	1.75/2 mm
No 10	1.25/1.5 mm
No 15	1.25/1.5 mm
No 20	1/1.25 mm
No 30	1/1.25 mm
No 40	1 mm
No 50	1 mm
No 60	0.75 mm
No 80	0.60 mm
No 100	0.60 mm

Yarn weight category	Super fine	Fine	Light	Medium	Bulky	Super bulky
	1	2	3	4	5	6
Type of yarns in category	Sock	Sport	DK	Worsted	Chunky	Bulky
	Fingering	Baby	Light worsted	Afghan, aran	Craft, rug	Roving
Crochet gauge ranges	21–28 sts	16–20 sts	16–18 sts	12–16 sts	8–12 sts	5–9 sts
Recommended crochet hook in U.S. size	Steel hooks, B1 to E4	E4 to G6	G6 to J9	J9 to K10½	K10½ to M/N13	K10½ to M/N13 and larger
Recommended crochet hook in metric	2.25–3.5 mm	3.5–4.5 mm	4.5–5.5 mm	5.5–6.5 mm	6.5–9 mm	9 mm and larger

SCALE

It is important that you understand how the weight of a yarn can affect the scale of the crochet piece produced. For an example of this, note that the doily and the coasters in the photograph below were made to the same pattern instructions, but in different weights of yarn and using different size crochet hooks (see page 38 for the full project).

CALCULATING YARN AMOUNTS WHEN SUBSTITUTING YARN

A pattern will tell you how much yarn to buy for your project. If you change the type of yarn used, then you may also have to change the amount of yarn you purchase. This is because all yarns will achieve a different length in relation to their weight. For example, a 50g ball of DK wool may have as much as 131 yards (120 meters) of yarn, whereas a 50g ball of cotton may have as little as 87 yards (80 meters). To calculate how many balls of an alternative yarn to buy, work out the total meterage of the original yarn, then divide this by the meterage of one ball of your chosen alternative.

The doily and coasters (page 38) are a great example of how crocheting a design in different weights of yarn can affect the scale of the finished pieces.

HOLDING THE HOOK

One of the first steps in learning to crochet is to learn how to hold the hook and yarn correctly. You can hold the crochet hook in one of two ways—choose whichever feels more comfortable. Be careful not to hold the hook too tightly or hold it too close to the tip.

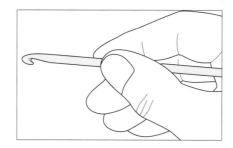

METHOD 1
Some people hold the crochet hook as if it were a pencil, with their thumb resting on the flat part of the hook and their index finger also resting on the top side of the hook.

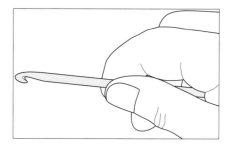

METHOD 2
Some people hold the crochet hook in the palm of their hand, with their thumb resting on the flat part of the hook and their remaining fingers holding the hook from the underside.

HOLDING THE YARN

One of the keys to producing a good crochet fabric is to achieve an even gauge (tension). Your left hand plays a vital role in this by tensioning the ball end of the yarn while you create your stitches. You will probably find your own way to achieve this, but in most cases the yarn is wrapped around, or held between, two fingers. Two examples are shown here.

Notes

To get started with crochet, choose a yarn that is smooth yet not too slippery—a good-quality cotton is ideal—and the compatible size crochet hook.

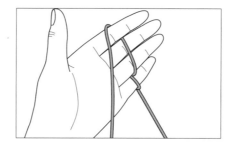

METHOD 1
Leaving a length of yarn about 4" (10 cm) from the loop on the hook, wrap the yarn around the little finger of your left hand, across the inside of your two middle fingers and then behind your index finger and to the front, leaving it to rest on your index finger.

TENSIONING THE TAIL
You need to regulate the tension of the yarn's tail end, or you will end up crocheting in mid-air. Use the middle finger and thumb of your left hand to pull gently on the tail end of yarn by pinching it just below the hook.

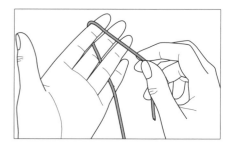

METHOD 2
Leaving a length of yarn about 4" (10 cm) from the loop on the hook, weave the yarn around the fingers of your left hand, starting with your little finger and ending with the yarn sitting behind your index finger and to the front, leaving it to rest on your index finger.

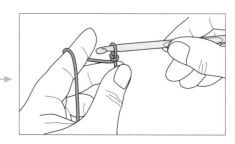

Basic crochet stitches

This section will get you started on making the most commonly used crochet stitches. Each stitch is made by forming a loop of yarn and drawing this loop through existing loops. It's much more straightforward than you might imagine.

U.S./U.K. CROCHET TERMS

Crochet terms in the U.S. and the U.K. are often different; most confusion arises when the same term is used to refer to completely different things. This book uses U.S. crochet terms and names for stitches, but when first introducing the stitching techniques

we have included the U.K. term in brackets, because understanding these differences will be useful to you as you start to use patterns more and more. The table, right, outlines the main differences. For more information, see Working from patterns (page 6).

U.S.		U.K.	
Slip stitch	sl st	Slip stitch	ss
Single crochet	sc	Double crochet	dc
Half double crochet	hdc	Half treble crochet	htr
Double crochet	dc	Treble crochet	tr
Treble crochet	tr	Double treble crochet	dtr

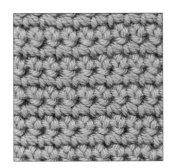

Repeated rows of single crochet (U.K. double crochet).

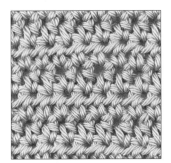

Repeated rows of half double crochet (U.K. half treble crochet).

Repeated rows of double crochet (U.K. treble crochet).

Repeated rows of treble crochet (U.K. double treble crochet).

MAKING A SLIP KNOT

In order to start crocheting you need to have a starting stitch on the hook. This is achieved by making a slip knot.

Notes

The pattern instructions may sometimes suggest you leave a tail end of a certain length; this is often the case when you are required to sew together pieces in a design made up of different parts.

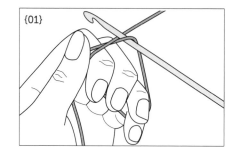

{01}

Leaving a tail end of about 4" (10 cm), make a loop in the yarn by wrapping it once around the fingers of your left hand. Pass the tip of the crochet hook through the loop and over the ball end of the yarn with the hook facing down.

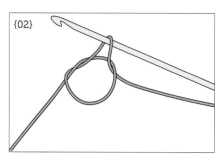

{02}

Use the hook to catch the ball end of yarn and pull it back through the loop. Keeping the new stitch on the hook, slip the loop from your left hand.

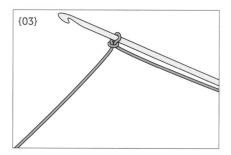

{03}

Pull gently on the tail end of yarn to tighten the slip knot around the hook.

WORKING THE FOUNDATION CHAIN
STITCH ABBREVIATION: CH

Crochet nearly always starts with a series of chain stitches. These stitches form the basis of the work and are equivalent to the "cast on" used in knitting. You may find that you struggle to keep an even gauge (tension) at first, but it is important to keep the chains even and not to make them too tight or loose.

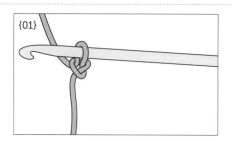

{01}

Place a slip knot on the hook and hold it in the right hand. Hold the yarn in the left hand, using your preferred method, and at the same time keep a good tension on the tail end of the yarn. With the yarn sitting to the reverse of the hook, turn the hook so that it is facing away from you.

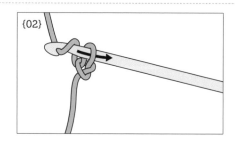

{02}

Push the crochet hook against the yarn, then rotate the hook in a counter-clockwise direction in order to catch the yarn around the hook, finishing the step with the hook facing down. Draw the yarn through the slip knot or the loop on the hook.

COUNTING CHAINS

When working from a pattern you will be asked to work a given number of chain stitches, so it is important that you can recognize the formation of each chain stitch, in order to be able to count the number of stitches correctly.

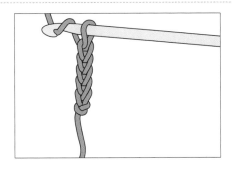

The front of the chain stitch looks like a series of V shapes made by the yarn. Each V is a chain loop sitting between a chain loop above and a chain loop below. The first chain at the beginning will have the slip knot sitting directly underneath it. The surface of the chain is smooth on this side. Stitches should be counted from this side of the chain where possible.

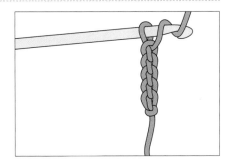

The reverse of the chain has a row of bumps that have been created by the yarn. These bumps sit behind the V and run in a vertical direction from the beginning of the chain up to the hook. The surface of the reverse of the chain is more textural than the front side.

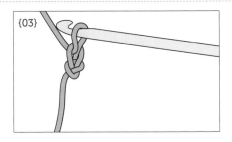

{03}

Rotate the hook clockwise so that it is left facing up and the new stitch is resting on the hook.

Notes

For the sake of clarity, the fingers tensioning the tail end of the yarn are not shown in the illustrations above and those that follow, but the yarn should be kept under tension at all times.

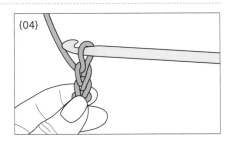

{04}

Repeat to create more chain stitches. You will need to reposition the tensioning fingers of your left hand every couple of stitches to ensure a good tension on the yarn.

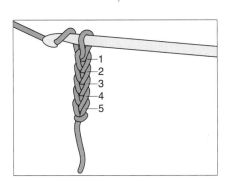

When counting the chain stitches you do not count the stitch that sits on the hook. This is because a loop will remain on the hook up until the moment you fasten off. When creating a large number of chains it may be a good idea to use stitch markers at a predetermined interval, say every ten or twenty stitches, to make counting easier.

WORKING INTO THE FOUNDATION CHAIN

To create a crochet fabric, stitches are worked into the foundation chain to create the first row. (There are several ways of doing this and three are given here.) Subsequent rows are then usually worked into the top of the previous row.

Notes

The first row can be tricky because you are working into the foundation chain, not into stitches. If the foundation chain is too tight, try working it in a larger size hook and change back to the hook size recommended in the pattern after you have worked the chain.

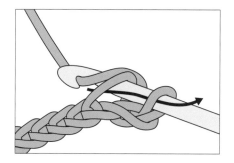

METHOD 1

You can place your hook into the top side of the chain, thus working over just one yarn. This method is easiest for the beginner, although it results in a rather loose edge.

METHOD 3

For a stronger, neater edge, you can work your foundation row into the yarn bumps at the reverse of the foundation chain. This can be a little tricky, but creates a nice effect, where the foundation edge is clearly visible on the right side.

METHOD 2

Alternatively, you may decide to place your hook into the lower part of the chain, thus working over two yarns.

TURNING CHAINS

When working crochet in rows or rounds, you will need to work a specific number of extra chains at the beginning of each row or round to bring the hook up to the correct height for the stitch to be worked on the following row. When working on a flat piece of crochet, the chains created at the end of a row are referred to as turning chains.

U.S.		U.K.
Single crochet	1 chain	Double crochet
Half double crochet	2 chains	Half treble crochet
Double crochet	3 chains	Treble crochet
Treble crochet	4 chains	Double treble crochet

Notes

Each crochet stitch has a suggested number of chains that should take your hook to the correct height for the row. However, if you find that the chain is either creating a loop, or appears to be pulling the subsequent stitches too tight, you may need to change the number of chain stitches worked.

→

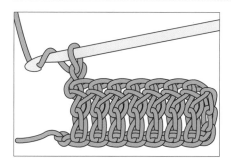

SINGLE CROCHET
[U.K. DOUBLE CROCHET]

This is the shortest of the crochet stitches and requires just 1 turning chain at the beginning of a row. Note: the turning chain is not counted as part of the overall stitch count.

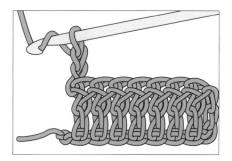

HALF DOUBLE CROCHET
[U.K. HALF TREBLE CROCHET]

The next tallest stitch requires 2 turning chains at the beginning of a row. Note: the turning chain is not counted as part of the overall stitch count.

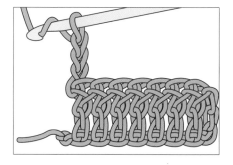

DOUBLE CROCHET
[U.K. TREBLE CROCHET]

This requires 3 turning chains at the beginning of a row. When working taller stitches, such as double crochet, the turning chain is counted as the first stitch of the row. For example, the written pattern may say: 3ch (counts as 1dc); this means that you work 3 chain stitches to get you to the height of the row and that the 3 chains will then subsequently count as the equivalent of one double crochet stitch.

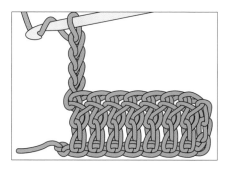

TREBLE CROCHET
[U.K. DOUBLE TREBLE CROCHET]

This requires 4 turning chains at the beginning of a row. As with double crochet, the turning chain counts as the first stitch of the row.

WORKING ADDITIONAL CHAINS

In some cases, you may find that the chain count is longer than the stitch height. This could be because the chain has to travel not only in a vertical direction to create the height of the row, but also in a horizontal direction to travel along the row. For example, the written pattern may say: 5ch (counts as 1dc plus 2ch). This would mean that three of the chain stitches are worked to replicate a double crochet, while the remaining 2ch are made in order to travel along the row.

WORKING THE FINAL STITCH

At the end of the row or round you will need to work your final stitch into the top of the turning or starting chain of the previous row. The top of the chain will look different from the other stitches and will not always have a clear gap in which to place your hook. Failure to work a stitch into the top of the turning or starting chain (where required) will mean that you will not achieve the correct stitch count.

Notes

When working in the round with the same side always facing, the chain created at the beginning of the round to get the hook to the height of the next stitch is sometimes referred to as a starting chain. In the case of a turning chain the work is turned, so alternate sides of the work face you.

WORKING A SLIP STITCH

STITCH ABBREVIATION: SL ST (U.K. SS)

Slip stitch or slipped stitch is most commonly used in order to travel from one point in your crochet to another, or to complete a row at the end of a round. This stitch adds very little height to the work and is unlikely to be used to produce a whole fabric.

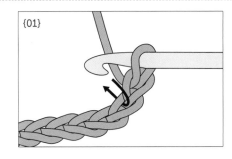

To work a slip stitch into the foundation chain, insert the hook into the second chain from the hook.

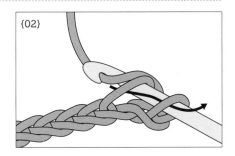

Pass the hook under the yarn so that it crosses over the hook and draw it through both the chain and the loop on the crochet hook.

WORKING SINGLE CROCHET
(U.K. DOUBLE CROCHET)

STITCH ABBREVIATION: SC (U.K. DC)

Single crochet is the shortest crochet stitch. It is hard-wearing and durable and the fabric produced has a dense, sturdy feel. It is a very good stitch to use for items for the home such as cushion covers and blankets.

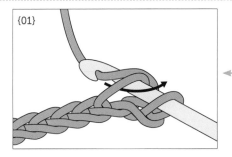

Work the foundation chain to the required length and insert your hook into the second chain from the hook. Draw the yarn around the hook and through the chain so that there are two loops on the crochet hook.

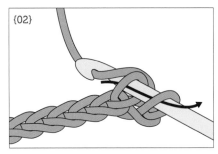

Catch the yarn around the hook again and draw the yarn through both loops on the crochet hook.

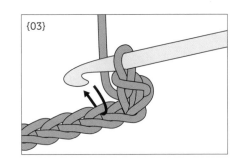

One complete single crochet stitch has been made. To continue, place the hook into the next foundation chain.

WORKING IN SC ROWS

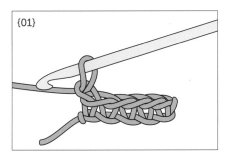

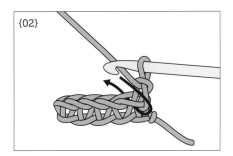

Once you have completed your first row, you are ready to continue to work your fabric. The first row is always the hardest, with subsequent rows much easier to work. At the end of the first row, work 1 chain to make the turning chain.

Turn the work so that the back is facing and insert the hook under the whole of the first stitch below the top loops. (This is the final stitch of the previous row and looks like a V shape running along the top of the piece of crochet.) Now continue to work single crochet stitches to the end of the row.

The Kindle cover (pages 74–75) is worked in rows of single crochet. This creates a dense and sturdy fabric that will help to protect the gadget within.

COUNTING STITCHES

To produce a good standard of crochet fabric, you must remember to count your stitches regularly. It is a good idea to count them at the end of every row. With the right side facing you will see that there is the appearance of a chain of V shapes running along the top of your first (or subsequent) row of single crochet. This looks much like the foundation chain, but it now has a series of V-shaped stitches sitting underneath.

To count the stitches, count from the hook down to the end of the row, making sure that you do not count the stitch on the hook. The stitch at the very beginning of the row may be sitting in a slightly vertical direction.

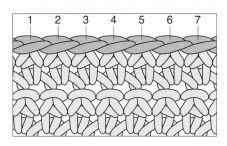

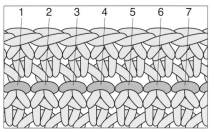

WORKING HALF DOUBLE CROCHET
(U.K. HALF TREBLE CROCHET)
STITCH ABBREVIATION: HDC (U.K. HTR)

Half way in height between single and double crochet, this stitch produces a firm and durable fabric. It is often used in conjunction with other stitches when making variegated patterns or motifs.

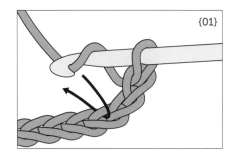

{01}

Work the foundation chain to the required length. Wrap the yarn around the hook before inserting the hook into the third chain from the hook.

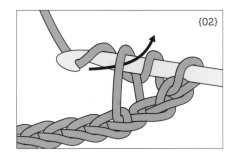

{02}

Wrap the yarn around the hook again and draw it through the chain so that there are three loops on the hook.

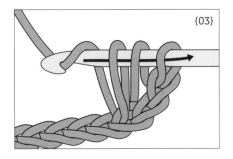

{03}

Catch the yarn around the hook once more and draw through all the loops on the hook. When drawing the yarn through three loops, take care not to split the yarn. Making sure that your hook is facing downward and that your stitches are not too tight should make this step of the stitch easier.

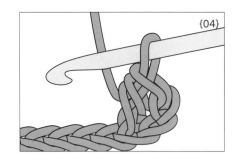

{04}

One complete half double crochet stitch has been made.

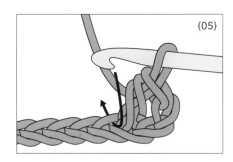

{05}

To continue, wrap the yarn around the hook, place hook into next chain and repeat from step 2.

WORKING IN HDC ROWS

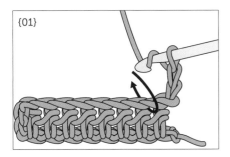

{01}

At the end of the row, work 2 chains for the turning chain and turn the work. For the first stitch of the new row, insert the hook into the stitch to the left of the turning chain. (This is the penultimate stitch of the previous row.) Now continue to work half double crochet stitches to the end of the row.

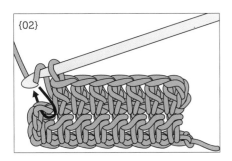

{02}

At the end of the row, work the final stitch into the top of the turning chain of the previous row.

The lattice edging version of the Baby blankets (page 27) is worked by combining half double stitches with chain to create the mesh-like lattice pattern.

WORKING DOUBLE CROCHET
(U.K. TREBLE CROCHET)
STITCH ABBREVIATION: DC (U.K. TR)

This stitch produces a more open and softer fabric than single crochet. The stitches produced appear like posts leading up from the previous row. Because it produces these longer stitches, this is quite a speedy stitch to complete once mastered.

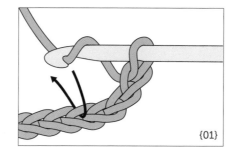

{01}

Work the foundation chain to the required length. Wrap the yarn around the hook once, then insert the hook into the fourth chain from the hook.

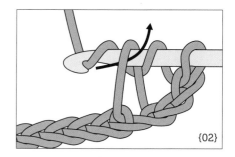

{02}

Wrap the yarn around the hook again and draw the yarn through the chain stitch so that there are three loops on the hook.

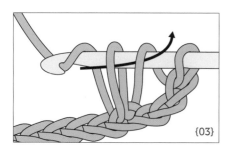

{03}

Wrap the yarn around the hook again and draw it through the first two loops on the hook.

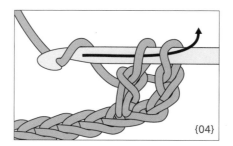

{04}

Catch the yarn again and draw it through the two remaining loops on the hook.

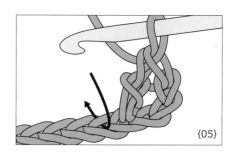

{05}

The stitch is now completed and two double crochet stitches have been created. Wrap the yarn around the hook, and place the hook into the next foundation chain to continue to work double crochet stitches to the end of the row.

WORKING IN DC ROWS

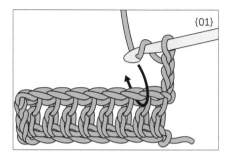
{01}

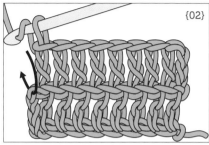
{02}

At the end of the first row, work 3 chain stitches for the turning chain and turn the work. Wrap the yarn around the hook, insert the hook under the top loops of the second stitch to the left of the turning chain and make a double crochet stitch.

Continue to work a double crochet stitch into each stitch of the previous row. Work the final stitch into the top of the turning chain created on the previous row.

COUNTING STITCHES

With the right side facing you will see that there is a row of "post" stitches leading from the top of your first (or subsequent) row of stitches. To count the stitches, count the posts from the hook down to the end of the row. The stitch at the very beginning of the row is the turning chain and is counted as a stitch.

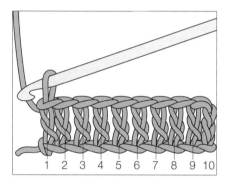

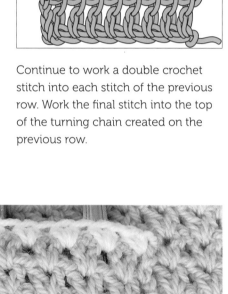

The placemats (pages 12–15) are created by working rows of double crochet. In this case, they are arranged into V-stitch groups (two doubles are worked into one space with a chain stitch in between).

WORKING TREBLE CROCHET
(U.K. DOUBLE TREBLE CROCHET)
STITCH ABBREVIATION: TR (U.K. DTR)

This stitch is often used in conjunction with other stitches when making variegated patterns or motifs.

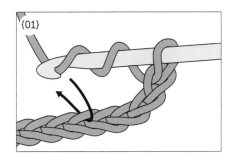

{01}

Work the foundation chain to the required length. Wrap the yarn around the hook twice, then insert the hook into the fifth chain from the hook.

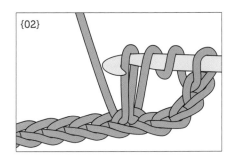

{02}

Wrap the yarn around the hook again and draw the yarn through the chain stitch so that there are four loops on the hook as seen in the illustration.

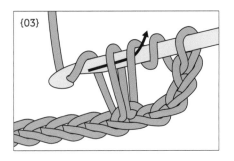

{03}

Wrap the yarn around the hook again and draw through the first two loops on the crochet hook—three loops will be left on the hook.

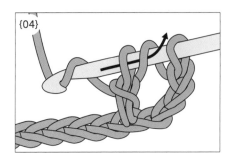

{04}

Catch the yarn again and draw through the next two loops to leave two loops on the crochet hook.

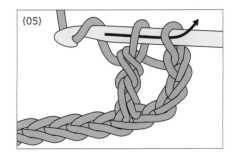

{05}

Wrap the yarn around the hook one last time and draw it through the remaining two loops on the crochet hook.

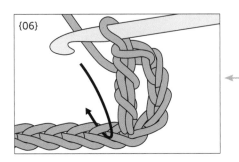

{06}

The stitch is now completed and two treble crochet stitches have been created. Wrap the yarn around the hook and place the hook into the next foundation chain to continue to work treble crochet stitches to the end of the row.

WORKING IN TR ROWS

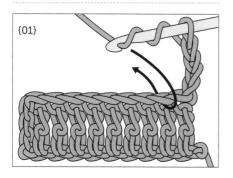

{01}

At the end of the first row, work 4 chain stitches for the turning chain and turn the work. Wrap the yarn around the hook, insert the hook under the top two loops of the second stitch to the left of the turning chain (this is the penultimate stitch of the previous row) and make a treble crochet stitch.

{02}

Continue to work a treble crochet stitch into each stitch of the previous row. Work the final stitch into the top of the turning chain created on the previous row.

WORKING TALLER STITCHES

Based on what you already know you can form taller stitches. For each subsequent "height" of stitch, you just need to wrap the yarn around the hook one more time.

Most crochet stitches produce what is referred to as a "post," which is the vertical part of the stitch that leads from the previous row. The length of the post of the stitch will vary, depending on how many times you wrap the yarn around the hook before you begin the process of working into the previous row or chain. The more times you wrap the yarn, the more times you repeat the process of drawing the yarn through the loops on the hook. To make taller stitches, refer to the useful table below.

KEEPING THE CORRECT STITCH COUNT

When working stitches with a long post it is very common to get a decreasing stitch count and end up with a piece of work rather more triangular in shape than rectangular. The usual reason for this is that the final stitch of the row has not been worked into the top of the turning chain made at the beginning of the previous row. To keep the stitch count correct, always count your stitches at the end of every row and be sure to work the final stitch into the top of the turning chain.

U.S.	U.K.	Turning Chain	Wrap Yarn
Double treble (dtr)	Treble treble (trtr)	5 chains	3 times
Triple triple (trtr)	Quadruple treble (quad tr)	6 chains	4 times
Quadruple treble (quad tr)	Quintuple treble (quintr)	7 chains	5 times
Quintuple treble (quintr)	Sextuple treble (sextr)	8 chains	6 times

Joining a new yarn

There are various ways of joining in a new yarn, depending on which stitch you are using and whether you are working a flat fabric with repeated rows, working in the round, or on a motif/block.

JOINING IN YARN USING SLIP STITCH

This method can be used for any stitch, but is best worked at the beginning of a row and not when working in the round.

Fasten off the yarn (see page 136). Place a slip knot made from the new yarn on the hook. Place hook through the first stitch of the row, wrap the new yarn around the hook and draw it through all the loops on the hook to create a slip stitch. Continue to work with the new yarn. When the fabric is complete, undo the slip knot and sew in the yarn end.

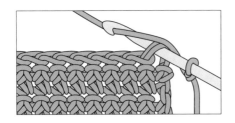

JOINING IN YARN USING SINGLE CROCHET

Use these methods of joining in a new yarn at the end or the middle of a row when working on a flat piece of fabric.

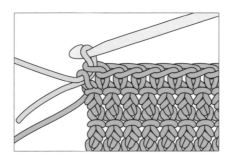

END OF ROW

In your final stitch of the row work through the stitch until the final step of the stitch, thus leaving two loops on the hook. Wrap the new yarn around the hook and draw through the two loops.

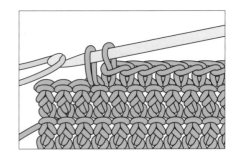

MID-WAY THROUGH ROW

Join in the new yarn where the pattern indicates by working through the stitch until the final step of the stitch, thus leaving two loops on the hook. Wrap the new yarn around the hook and draw through the two loops. Continue to work in new yarn as required.

JOINING IN YARN USING OTHER STITCHES

When using stitches that create a post as part of their formation—such as double crochet—use the following methods.

Notes

When working on a flat piece, always try to join a new yarn on the final stitch of a row in preparation for use on the first stitch of the following row. When joining a new yarn part way through a row, it is important to create a really neat join, otherwise the yarn change could be obvious and may spoil the outcome of your piece.

Joining in new yarn neatly is a necessity when working in narrow stripes, as for the iPod cover (page 73).

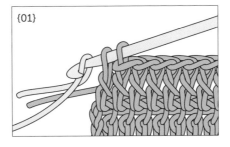

{01}

END OF ROW
On your final stitch, work through the stitch until the final step of the stitch, with the last two loops on the hook. Wrap the new yarn around the hook and draw through the two loops.

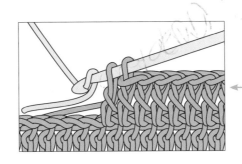

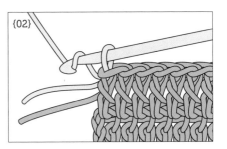

{02}

Turn and work the following row with the new yarn. You may want to knot the two yarn ends together to prevent them from slipping through the stitch and unraveling, but always undo the knot before sewing in the yarn ends.

MID-WAY THROUGH ROW
When joining mid-row, join in the new yarn where the pattern indicates by working through the stitch until the final step of the stitch, with the last two loops on the hook. Wrap the new yarn around the hook and draw through the two loops. Continue to work in new yarn as required.

Working in the round

Many crochet motifs are created by working in the round (starting at the center and working outward). This often means that there is no need to turn your work at the end of each round, so you constantly have one side of the work facing you.

MAKING A RING USING A CHAIN

To start your circular motif, you need to create a base of chain stitches to work around.

{01}

Make the required number of chain stitches; the more chains made at the start, the larger the hole at the center of the motif will be.

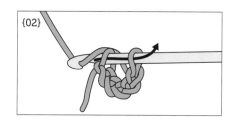
{02}

Join the chain using a slip stitch: to do this, insert the hook into the first chain made after the initial slip knot. Wrap the yarn around the hook and bring through all loops on the hook.

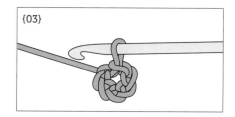
{03}

Tighten by pulling gently on the yarn. The foundation ring is now complete.

MAKING A YARN RING

Instead of using a chain to make your ring base, you can choose to make a yarn ring. This method should not be used with slippery yarns as they can loosen over time.

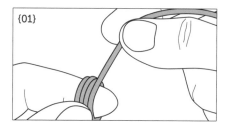
{01}

Wind the yarn several times around your left index finger, holding the yarn end securely between the finger and your thumb.

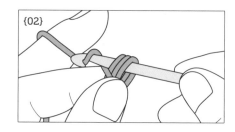
{02}

Carefully slip the yarn ring from your finger and onto the crochet hook. Wrap the yarn around the hook and draw through the center of the ring. Work the required number of chains to create the height of the chosen stitch.

WORKING STITCHES INTO THE CENTER OF THE RING

The central ring will be covered over by your first row of stitches, so it will not be visible once your piece is complete.

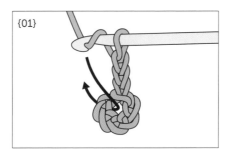

{01}

Make the central ring, then work the required number of chains to create the height of the stitch. The three chain stitches shown here will count as the first double crochet.

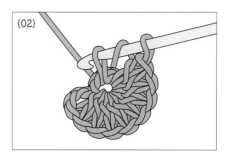

{02}

To create the next and each subsequent stitch, start by placing the hook into the center of the ring. Push the stitches around the central ring to bunch them up and make room for all the stitches required. Count the stitches at the end of the round, remembering that the starting chain could count as a stitch.

Notes

Often the density of the stitches made into the starting ring will be sufficient to cover up the gap in the center of the ring. However, if you find you have a visible gap that you don't want, try starting off with a magic loop instead (see overleaf).

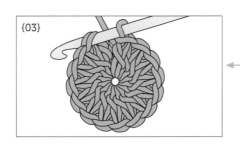

{03}

When the round is complete, join the last stitch to the top of the first stitch using a slip stitch.

NEATENING A SLIP STITCH AT THE END OF A ROUND

If the slip stitch made at the end of the round is loose or a little sloppy it can be quite obvious and can form a repeated, inconsistent stitch on the right side of the piece. You can use the following method to avoid this. Remove the hook from the last stitch worked and place on a stitch marker. From the reverse of the piece, insert the hook through the stitch that you intend to make the slip stitch into. Place the held stitch back on the hook and draw through the stitch to the reverse side.

Keeping your slip stitches neat and even will help you to create crisp circular motifs.

THE MAGIC LOOP METHOD OF STARTING A ROUND

The magic loop (also known as the magic circle) is an alternative way of starting off a piece of crochet to be worked in the round while avoiding being left with a gap in the center circle. Rather than starting off with a length of foundation chain that is joined into a ring ready for the first row of crochet stitches, you start off with a simple loop of yarn.

Notes

The magic loop creates an adjustable ring that can be drawn up tight after the first row of crochet has been completed to close the gap. This is useful for items where you want to create a tight, dense texture— for example for toys that you will eventually fill with stuffing.

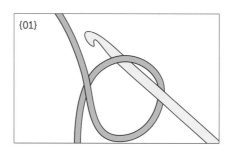

{01}

Start by making a loop in the working end of the yarn. Leave a fairly long tail (6"–8"/15–20.5 cm) so you have plenty to work with. Pinch the join of the loop together with the fingers of your left hand. The diameter of the loop should be about ¾"–1¼" (2–3.2 cm).

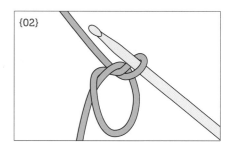

{02}

Insert the hook from right to left through the loop to pick up the working end of the yarn and make 1ch (this does not count as a stitch).

{03}

Make the first stitch into the loop (this example shows single crochet). You need to insert the hook under both strands of yarn—the yarn that forms the loop and the yarn that forms the hanging tail—before picking up the working yarn and pulling it through.

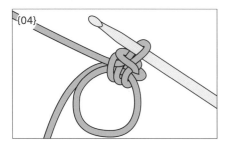

{04}

First single crochet stitch made.

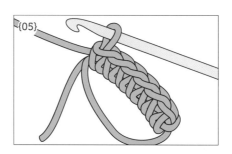

{05}

Continue until you have made as many stitches as are required.

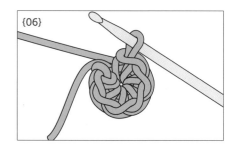

{06}

Pull on the tail end of the yarn to close the central gap. Join the round with a slip stitch into the first stitch.

Mollie MAKES CROCHET

WORKING THE NEXT (SECOND) ROUND

When working a flat motif you must create a flat and even circle, otherwise you will end up with a tube. You will need to increase the number of stitches used on every new round by working more than one new stitch into all or some stitches on the previous round.

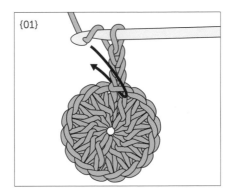

{01}

Work the required number of chain stitches to create the stitch height. The three chain stitches shown here count as the first double crochet. Work the first stitch into the base of the chain.

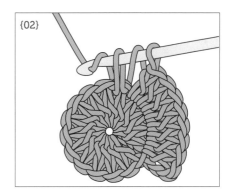

{02}

Work two stitches into every stitch of the previous round. When the round is complete, join the last stitch to the top of the first stitch using a slip stitch.

Notes

As a general rule, on the first increase round you will be asked to work two stitches into every stitch of the previous round.

The crisp circular shape of the round pot holder (page 58) is created by working regular increases.

INCREASING AROUND THE RING

After the first row of increasing, you will need to add new stitches less frequently. You may find that you are asked to work an increase into one stitch of the previous round and then work one or two single stitches before repeating the increase once more. Sometimes the increases are more spread out, and you may even be asked to work more than two stitches into a stitch on the previous round to achieve the correct stitch count.

When working from a chart, an increase is indicated by two or three stitches sitting in a V- or W-formation above a single stitch in the row below.

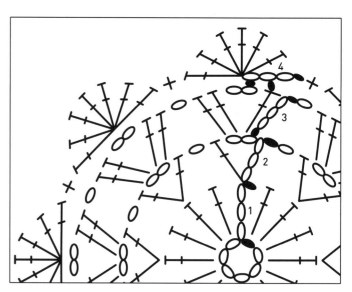

KEEPING ROUNDS FLAT

When working in the round, it is quite common for the piece to become a little bit frilly. This could be because you have increased too many times, or are not working to the correct gauge (tension). If you are following a pattern and find that your motifs are consistently coming out wavy, try using a smaller hook.

A circular motif that has become frilly.

A perfectly flat circular motif.

JOINING IN NEW YARN

You could choose to use any of the methods shown on pages 100–101 to join in a new yarn when working in the round or on a block or motif. However, you will get a much neater appearance if you join in the new yarn once you have fastened off the previous yarn.

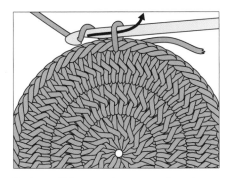

Fasten off the previous yarn. Insert hook into the final stitch. Make the required number of chains to work the chosen stitch, then continue to work in the new yarn as required.

WORKING A MULTICOLOR MOTIF

When working a motif where the color is changed on every row, you can achieve a much neater appearance by fastening off one color then rejoining another in a different position.

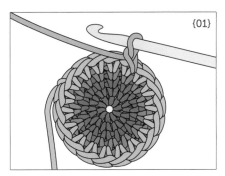

{01}

At the end of the first round, work a slip stitch into the first stitch of the row. Cut the yarn and fasten off. Join the next color using a slip stitch at another point of the motif.

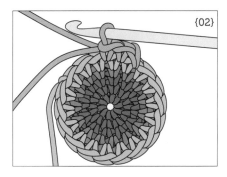

{02}

Work the required number of chains for the height of the stitch. Hold the tail end of yarn in line with the top of the last row and work the next few stitches over the top of it in order to weave it in.

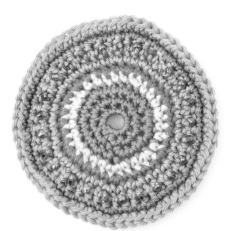

A circular motif in which the colors have been fastened off and rejoined at a different point.

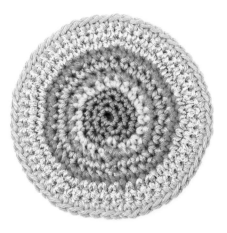

A circular motif where the colors have been joined in at the end of the round—note that the first stitch of the new color intrudes into the previous one.

Many crochet motifs start off with a circle of stitches made around a central chain—even sharp-edged shapes, such as squares and triangles, may have been started with a circle as a base. To create a more angular shape from a circle, you will need to learn how to create corners.

MAKING A SQUARE FROM A CENTRAL CHAIN

To work around a corner, you need to work more than one stitch into a space. In this example, the classic "granny square" is made with double crochet throughout.

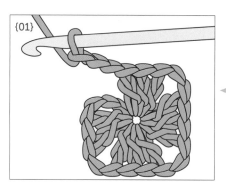

{01}

Make 6ch and join with a sl st to form a ring. Work 3ch to reach the height of the stitch (this will subsequently count as a stitch). Work 2 more stitches into the center of the ring. To create a corner, work 3ch. Work 3 stitches into the center of the ring. Repeat until four corners have been created. Work a sl st into the top of the 3ch.

{02}

On the second and subsequent rounds, join the new color in at a corner space. This time, work 3 sts, 3ch, 3 sts, 1ch into the corner made on the previous round.

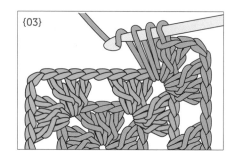

{03}

As the granny square gets bigger, work a single block of 3 sts into the chain space on the row below, in order to travel along the block between the corners.

Opposite: The classic granny square—a very commonly found motif in crochet—is created from an initial chain-stitch ring.

MAKING A SQUARE FROM A ROUND

Here an existing round motif is shown with no chain corners so the piece retains its circular shape. To make it square, you must ensure that the number of stitches already created is divisible by four to achieve the correct number of corners at an equal spacing.

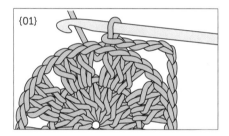

Work a series of chain spaces around the piece to allow the next row to be worked. Make a larger chain space at each of the four corners.

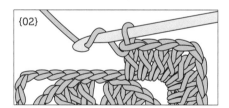

On the subsequent round, work small groups of stitches in line with the sides of the block then a larger multiple of stitches into the corner—it is a good idea to make this an uneven number such as 3, 5, or 7, depending on the size of the block and the depth of the post of the stitch.

MAKING CORNERS ON OTHER BLOCKS

If you are making a shape other than a square, you will need to create a different number of corners.

The motifs of the hexagon motif blanket (pages 64–67) start off with circular rounds. The final round adds six corners to make the hexagonal shape.

WORKING HEXAGONAL OR OCTAGONAL SHAPES

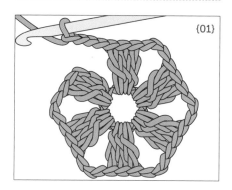

{01}

Start with a larger central ring to allow enough room for the corners on subsequent rounds. On the classic granny hexagon, work as for the granny square (see page 108), repeating corners created by chains and groups of stitches around the initial ring, making sure that you achieve the correct number of corners for the shape.

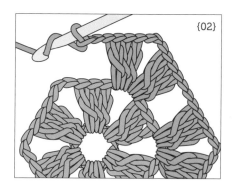

{02}

On the subsequent rounds, join the new color in at a corner space and work two groups of stitches joined by a chain to create the corner for the next round.

MAKING AN EXISTING CIRCULAR SHAPE INTO AN ANGULAR SHAPE

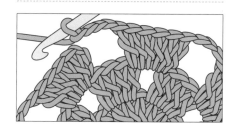

Work more than one round before you start to make the corners.

Notes

When working a granny square or hexagon you need to start each new color in a corner space. This will make it difficult to weave the yarn tail in as you work your next row, so you will have to sew it in (see pages 136–137). To make the piece neater, try to join the yarn in at a different corner on each round.

Making tubular shapes

One of the exciting things about the craft of crochet is that you can choose whether or not you want to produce a flat piece of fabric or a piece that forms a tube or cylinder. Tubular crochet can be used to make garments, mittens, socks, accessories and toys. When making a tube or cylindrical shape, each row of stitching is referred to as a round.

WORKING A SPIRAL CYLINDER

When using stitches with shallow posts—such as single crochet—you can work the cylinder in a spiral. Working in this stitch means that you do not need to complete each round with a slip stitch or start a round with a chain to reach the height of the stitch

A cylinder in single crochet.

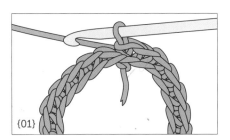

{01}

Make a chain to the required length, making sure it is not twisted. Work a slip stitch into the first stitch to form a ring. Work one round of stitches into each chain. Join the round by working a slip stitch into the first stitch made.

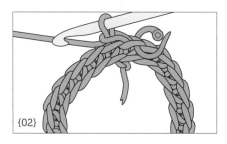

{02}

Insert a stitch marker into the last stitch made. Work another row, working a new stitch into every stitch of the previous round.

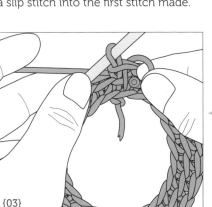

{03}

At the end of the round, do not work a slip stitch into the first stitch of the previous round but continue in a spiral by working into the first stitch of the round and replacing the marker in the new stitch to mark the end/beginning of the round. Continue in this way, replacing the marker at the end/beginning of each round until the piece is the required length.

Shaping crochet pieces

When making a garment, or following a crochet pattern—when working decorative stitches such as chevrons, for example—you may need to either increase or decrease the number of stitches in the row. Increasing and decreasing can be done either part way through a row, or at either end.

INCREASING STITCHES WITHIN A ROW

If the increasing is to be done part way through a row, the pattern will usually tell you exactly where you need to create more stitches. Increases can be made using any stitches. The illustrations here show one-stitch and two-stitch increases made in double crochet.

TO MAKE ONE EXTRA STITCH
Work to where the increase is required. Work 2 stitches into the next stitch.

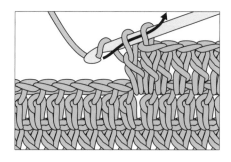

Detail of a one-stitch increase, in which two stitches have been made from one.

FOR MORE THAN ONE EXTRA STITCH
Work to where the increase is required. Work 3 (or more stitches) into the next stitch.

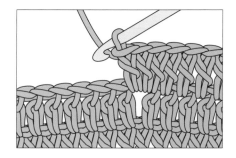

Detail of a two-stitch increase, in which three stitches have been made from one.

DECREASING STITCHES WITHIN A ROW

To decrease by one stitch within a row, work to where the decrease is required, as noted in the pattern. Decreases can be made using any stitches. The illustration here shows a decrease made in single crochet.

{01}

Work an incomplete stitch, by stopping before the last step of each stitch, work into the next 2 stitches to leave three loops on the hook.

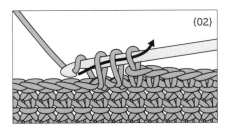

Wrap the yarn around the hook and draw through all the loops.

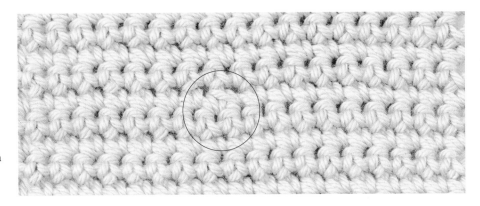

Detail of a one-stitch decrease, in which two stitches have been reduced to one, worked over single crochet fabric.

INCREASING STITCHES ON THE RIGHT-HAND SIDE OF THE FABRIC

To increase on the right-hand side of the fabric, you will need to add an area of chain stitch in which to work the subsequent row. This chain is added at the end of a reverse-side row.

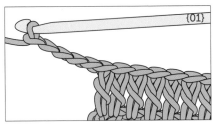

Work to the end of the reverse-side row. Make the required number of chains, remembering to add enough to allow for any turning chains needed.

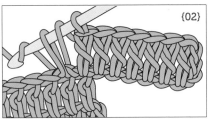

Turn and work the next row of stitches into the chain and then into the subsequent stitches of the previous row.

Increasing on the right-hand side.

INCREASING STITCHES ON THE LEFT-HAND SIDE OF THE FABRIC

When using a stitch with a long post, you may need to create the shaping at the beginning and the end of the same row, to avoid shaping on the left side being a row higher.

Work to the last few stitches of the row. Remove the working stitch from the crochet hook and place on a stitch holder. Join a length of yarn to the final stitch of the row and work the required number of chain stitches. Fasten off the chain. Insert the hook back into the held stitch and work to the end of the row, working the final few stitches into the previous row, then subsequent stitches into the added chain.

Increasing on the left-hand side.

REVERSE SHAPING

Crochet patterns have set ways in which they communicate instructions. To save space, many patterns will ask you to "work as set", for example, so that each row of the pattern does not need to be written. One instruction that often confuses is to "reverse shaping".

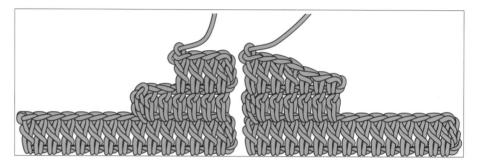

To reverse the shaping, you will first have worked a piece from the pattern, but you now need to work a second piece as a mirror image of the first. This will mean working the shaping as instructed for the first piece, but at the opposite end of the row. A way to keep track of where you are is to draw out the shape required on a piece of paper.

GRADUAL SHAPING

When using a stitch with a long post, shaping can look a little clumsy, with the edges of the crochet fabric stepped. You may prefer to work gradual shaping in order to achieve a slope instead.

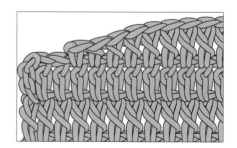

Work a sequence of stitches with smaller posts into the first few stitches, as shown in this illustration.

Decorative stitches

Once you know the crochet basics, you can start to make more decorative stitches rather than just working in rows. Incorporating increases and decreases, for example, means you can work waves and chevrons, while working into rows below allows you to make the eye-catching spike stitch.

SPIKE STITCHES

These stitches are sometimes referred to as "dropped" stitches and are made by working over the top of stitches made on a previous row. This technique can be particularly effective when working in contrasting colors in a stripe formation, but it can also be attractive as a plain-colored fabric.

Notes

It can be quite difficult to identify where to insert the hook into the crochet fabric in order to make a spike stitch sit perfectly. It is a little tricky to achieve a perfect vertical spike stitch, so take your time and practice. Undo stitches that look skewed if need be.

WORKING A SPIKE STITCH USING SINGLE CROCHET

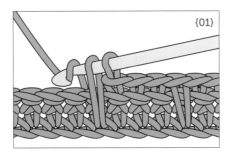

{01}

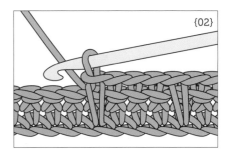

{02}

Work to where a spike stitch is required. From the front, count down a few rows (depending on how deep the spike stitch needs to be), then push the hook through the fabric to the reverse of the work, being careful not to split the yarn. Wrap the yarn around the hook, then draw through to the front of the work to form another loop on the hook.

Do not pull the loop tight, as this will cause the crochet to pucker. Wrap the yarn around the hook and complete the stitch.

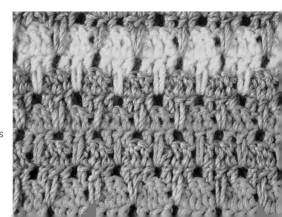

The Spike stitch iPad cozy (pages 42–44), worked in doubles, shows how striking this stitch can look when worked in vibrant, contrasting colors.

CHEVRON STITCHES

Chevron stitches are sometimes referred to as "ripple" stitches and are characterized by their distinctive zigzag pattern, created by a series of increases and decreases, often set on the foundation row and then repeated throughout.

CHEVRON MADE USING SINGLE CROCHET

This technique is for a basic chevron stitch.

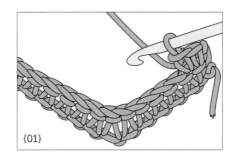

{01}

Make a chain to the required length, work a row of stitches into the chain. Work 2 stitches into the first stitch of the row.

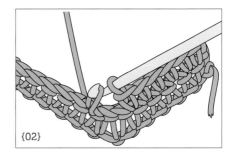

{02}

Work to where the decrease is required, *skip the next 2 stitches. Continue to work stitches into each stitch on the previous row.

A chevron made in single crochet.

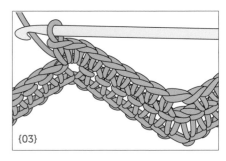

{03}

Work to where the increase is required, work 3 stitches into the next stitch. Continue to work stitches into each stitch on the previous row. Repeat from * to the end of the row. Work 2 stitches into the final stitch before turning to work the next row. Repeat on the next row.

CHEVRON MADE USING DOUBLE CROCHET

In order to keep the sides of the work neat and the stitch count correct, the chevron pattern made with stitches with a longer post may require a decrease or a slip stitch to be worked at the beginning of the row.

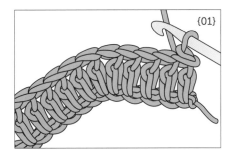

Work the first row, turn and work a slip stitch into the second stitch of the previous row. Work the turning chain.

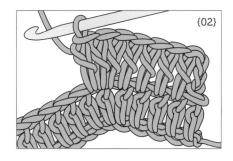

*Work to where the increase is required, work 3 stitches into the next stitch.

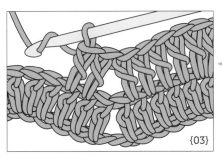

Work to where the decrease is required, skip the next 2 stitches. Continue to work stitches into the next sequence of stitches on the previous row. Repeat from * to the end of the row.

A chevron made in double crochet.

Notes

Chevrons are made by working corners at two repeated points in the piece. The top of the chevron is made by increasing, and the bottom by decreasing. The number of stitches between each point varies according to the individual design, but the stitch count usually remains constant throughout. It is a good idea to count your stitches at the end of every row. If you have lost stitches, you may need to increase into the first or last stitch of the row. It can be difficult to keep track of where you should be decreasing and increasing, so use stitch markers to identify the points of the chevron.

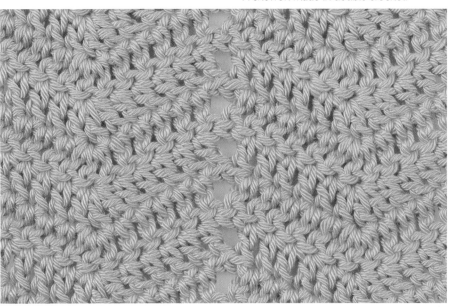

WAVE STITCH

A wave stitch is similar to a chevron in that stitches are increased to make a "hilltop" and decreased to make a "valley". However, a wave is less angular, with the decreases and increases made over more stitches. The technique shows wave stitch made using double crochet.

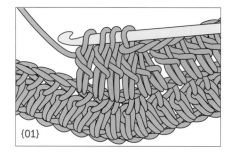

{01}

Work to where the decrease is required (this is the 6 stitches at the base of the valley, 3 either side of the central point). *Into the next 3 stitches work 3 incomplete stitches, leaving one loop remaining on the hook for each stitch as if working a cluster (see page 120). Work the 3 stitches together by drawing the yarn through the final loops. Repeat from * once more.

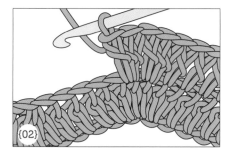

{02}

Work to where the increase is required (this is the central pair of stitches at the top of the previous wave). Work 3 stitches into each of these stitches.

Wave stitch in double crochet.

Wave stitch looks particularly effective worked in sequences of color.

RIDGE STITCHES

Create a line of yarn, or a ridge, by crocheting into just one loop along the top of a row using any stitch or combination of stitches. The ridge will be on either the right side or wrong side of every alternate row if you work continuously into one side of the stitch. If you want a ridge on just one side of the fabric on every row, alternate which side of the stitch you work through.

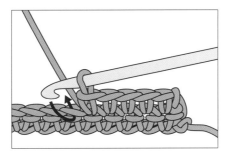

WORKING INTO THE FRONT OF A STITCH USING SINGLE CROCHET
Hold the crochet flat so that the stitches that run along the top of the previous row are clearly visible. Insert the hook through the front loop of the stitch on the previous row.

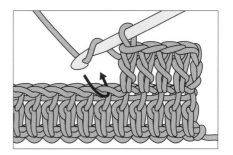

WORKING INTO THE FRONT OF A STITCH USING DOUBLE CROCHET
Hold the crochet flat so that the stitches that run along the top of the previous row are clearly visible. Insert the hook through the front loop of the stitch on the previous row.

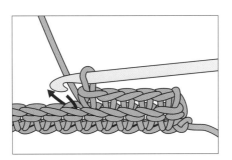

WORKING INTO THE BACK OF A STITCH USING SINGLE CROCHET
Hold the crochet flat so that the stitches that run along the top of the previous row are clearly visible. Insert the hook through the far loop of the stitch on the previous row.

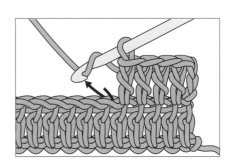

WORKING INTO THE BACK OF A STITCH USING DOUBLE CROCHET
Hold the crochet flat so that the stitches that run along the top of the previous row are clearly visible. Insert the hook through the far loop of the stitch on the previous row.

The flap of the Kindle cover (pages 74–75) is begun by working a row of single crochet stitches through the back loops to form a distinct fold line.

Textured stitches

A variety of textured stitches can be created in crochet. These stitches tend to stand proud of the surface of a crochet fabric (usually worked in rows of plain single or double crochet), and can add a three-dimensional touch to a crocheted item.

CLUSTERS

A cluster is made by working a series of incomplete stitches into either a sequence of single stitches or into a chain space to form a group of close-sitting stitches. On the final step of the stitch all the stitches are joined together to form one stitch. The directions here are given for working a two-stitch cluster made over two stitches using double crochet. Clusters are most effective when made using stitches with long posts.

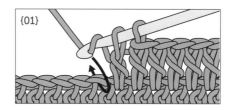

Wrap the yarn around the hook and work a stitch into the next stitch on the row, stopping before the last step of the stitch so that two loops remain on the hook.

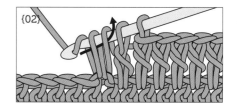

Work another stitch in the same way into the next stitch, or as directed, so that three loops remain on the hook.

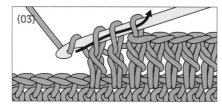

Wrap the yarn around the hook and draw through all the loops remaining on the hook to produce just one stitch.

WORKING A CLUSTER INTO A CHAIN SPACE

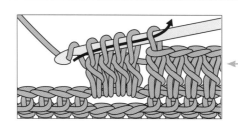

Work a series of incomplete stitches into the space created by a chain on the previous row. Finish by drawing the yarn through the stitches—a 4-stitch cluster is being shown here.

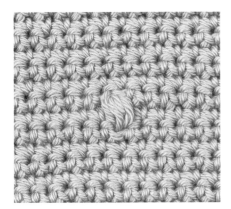

A puff stitch in double crochet on a single crochet base fabric.

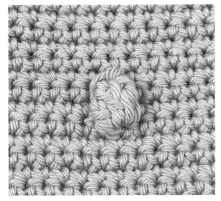

A five-stitch popcorn (see page 122) on a single crochet base fabric, for comparison.

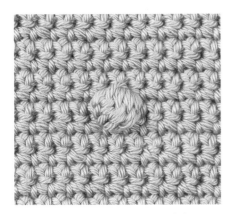

A five-stitch bobble (see page 123) on a single crochet base fabric, for comparison.

PUFF STITCH

Puff stitches are similar in appearance to both popcorns (see page 122) and bobbles (see page 123), but they are a little softer, with less definition than either. A puff stitch is made by working three or more stitches into the same stitch or space.

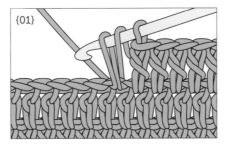

{01}

Wrap the yarn around the hook and draw through the stitch leaving three loops on the hook.

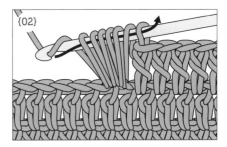

{02}

Repeat step 1 twice more, inserting the hook into the same stitch each time. (There are seven loops on the hook.) Wrap the yarn around the hook and draw through all the loops left on the hook.

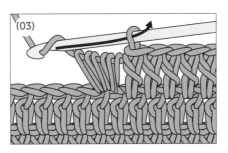

{03}

Wrap the yarn around the hook once more and draw through the stitch that remains on the hook, thus securing all the loops in place.

Notes

This sequence shows a puff stitch made using treble crochet. Work to where a puff stitch is required, then follow this technique.

POPCORN STITCH

A popcorn is made by working a group of stitches into one stitch or space, as for a puff stitch or bobble (see pages 121 and 123), but it differs from both in that it is made from complete groups of stitches, which are then joined together on the final step of the stitch. A popcorn is a relief stitch that works best when made using a stitch with a long post. It looks rather like a small pouch.

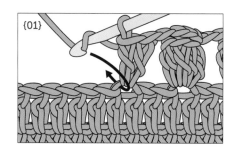

Work to where a popcorn is required. Skip 2 stitches on the previous row. Work a group of 5 stitches into the next stitch.

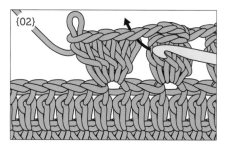

Remove the hook from the working stitch. Making sure that this stitch does not unravel, insert the hook into the top of the first stitch of the group of 5.

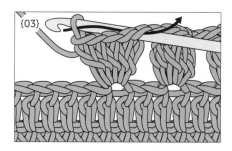

Place the working stitch back on the hook and draw it through the top of the first stitch of the group of 5. Wrap the yarn around the hook a final time and draw through the final stitch, thus securing the popcorn.

Notes

This sequence shows a basic five-stitch popcorn made using double crochet.

The popcorns on the Square pot holder (page 59) are made up of groups of seven double stitches.

BOBBLES

A bobble is a very sturdy stitch, which is made by working a group of stitches into one stitch or space (as for a puff stitch, or popcorn stitch). At the end of the process, the group of stitches are worked together to form just one stitch.

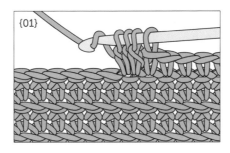

With the wrong side of the work facing, work to where a bobble is required. Work 3 incomplete stitches by leaving the last loop of each stitch on the crochet hook, so that four loops remain on the hook.

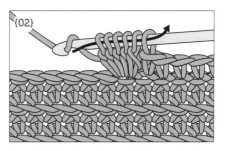

Work 2 more incomplete stitches, to leave six loops on the hook. Wrap the yarn around the hook and draw through all the loops on the hook.

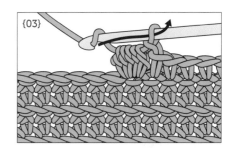

Wrap the yarn around the hook a final time and draw through the loop on the hook. Gently push the group of stitches through to the right side of the work.

Notes

This sequence shows a basic five-stitch bobble made using double crochet on a base of single crochet worked into the back of the stitch.

The bobbles on the iPad cover (pages 70–73) are made of double crochet stitches set against a fabric of single crochet.

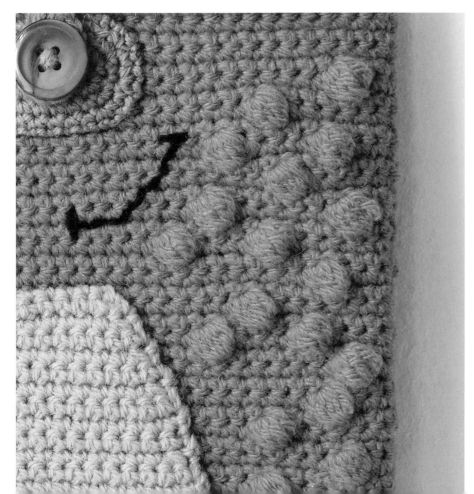

Lacy and open-work stitches

One of the most recognisable characteristics of crochet is its use in decorative, lacy and open stitches—testament to crochet's origins in mimicking very fine hand-knotted lace. Often such stitch patterns are built by working into chain spaces, or working between stitches.

SKIPPING STITCHES

In some cases a pattern may ask you to skip either one or a number of stitches, either to decrease the stitch count or to make a pattern repeat work.

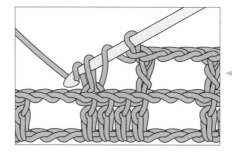

To skip the required number of stitches you will need to count the stitches on the previous row, then work your subsequent stitch into the first stitch beyond this stitch or group of stitches. This technique is often used in lace or open-work.

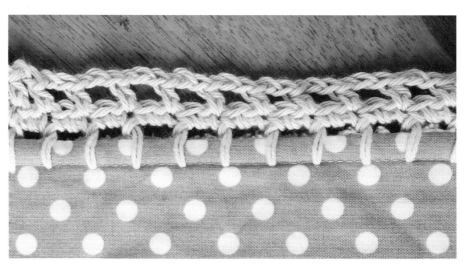

The mesh-like stitch pattern of the Baby blanket lattice edging (page 27) is created by skipping stitches on the previous round.

WORKING INTO SPACES CREATED BY STITCHES OR CHAIN

You may find that you are asked to work a stitch or group of stitches into a space (abbreviation sp) created on the previous row or round, as opposed to working into a stitch.

Many flower designs create the petal-like effect by working stitches into chain spaces.

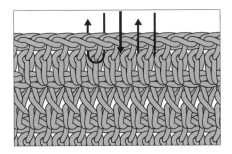

WORKING INTO SPACES CREATED BY STITCHES

To work into the space between two stitches when using stitches that create a post as part of their formation (such as double crochet) you will need to insert the hook into the gap that is formed between the two stitches—which is lower than the stitches running along the top of the piece, which join one stitch to the next.

WORKING INTO A SPACE CREATED BY A CHAIN

Insert the hook into the gap created by the chain and not into the individual stitches. You will see that this causes the stitches to wrap themselves around the chain and cover it.

Here the double crochet stitches are worked between stitches on the row below for a distinctive "off-set" look.

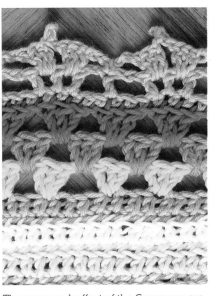

The open-work effect of the Granny square blanket edging (page 55) is achieved by making groups of stitches into chain spaces.

MESH STITCHES

A mesh fabric can be used as a background fabric for more textural stitches, and as it is a very open fabric, it works very well in lace patterns. It can be tricky to keep the stitch count correct so make sure that you count your stitches at the end of a row.

Basic mesh.

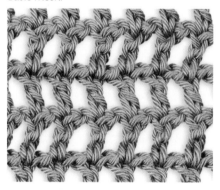

Basic off-set mesh: work your stitches into the gap between stitches.

BASIC MESH

To make a mesh you will need to use stitches with a long post. For a basic mesh, work your stitches into the stitch itself.

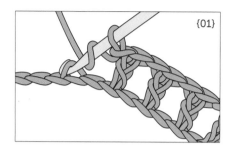

Work a row of stitches into the foundation chain, skipping 1ch and working 1ch between each stitch.

Insert the hook into the top of the stitch on the previous row. This will create a mesh where the stitches line up on every row.

OFF-SET MESH

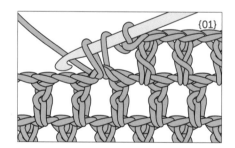

Work a row of stitches into the foundation chain, skipping 1ch and working 1ch between each stitch. On the subsequent row, insert the hook into the space made by the mesh pattern on the previous row.

The mesh pattern becomes off-set and there are fewer spaces into which to work stitches. Make an extra stitch at the end of the row into the top of the first stitch on the previous row to correct the stitch count.

TRELLIS PATTERN

Trellis stitch also works really effectively as a background for textural stitches and can look especially attractive when used in conjunction with a lace edging, for example.

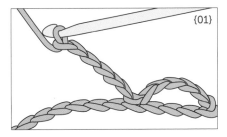

Chain spaces are created by working a series of chain loops that are about a third longer than the number of skipped chain stitches. The chain length can vary from pattern to pattern.

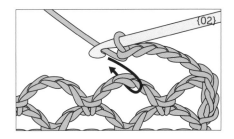

The last chain loop of the row is slightly shorter. The chain at the beginning of the row is then anchored into the space made by the chain on the previous row, using a slip stitch or other short-post stitch.

A sample of trellis.

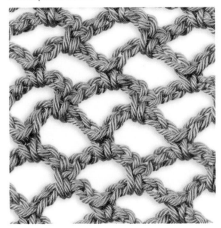

VARYING THE TRELLIS

When working a trellis you can choose how many chain stitches you wish to use between your securing stitches— the longer the chain you make, the larger the gaps in the trellis will be. You may also want to experiment creating irregular-sized spaces, thus working in a more free-form way.

The Lacy stripes bolster (pages 60–63) reveals the effectiveness of combining trellis stitch with groups of doubles to create a lacy pattern.

SHELLS AND FANS

Shell and fan stitches are made by working a group of stitches into one space or stitch. Because a group of stitches can take up more space than a single stitch, the stitches spread themselves out to create the appearance of a shell or a fan. Shells and fans are often used in conjunction with a mesh or trellis background to make intricate lace patterns.

Shells can look particularly effective worked in rounds of contrasting colors.

BASIC 3-STITCH SHELL USING DOUBLE CROCHET

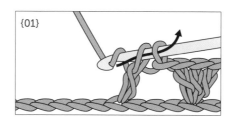

Work to where the shell is required, skip the number of chains/stitches stated in the pattern (here a skip of 3 chains). Work a stitch into the next chain/stitch.

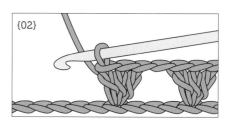

Work another 2 stitches into the same chain/stitch, thus completing a shell.

Basic three-stitch shell in double crochet.

Notes

A small group of stitches, such as three or four, is referred to as a shell. A large group of stitches, say five or seven, is referred to as a fan because it takes up more space than a shell.

In order to keep the stitch count correct it may be necessary to work a half-shell at the beginning or end of the row. To do this at the beginning of the row, work 2 stitches into the first stitch.

To do this at the end of the row, work 2 stitches into the final stitch of the row.

WORKING A WIDE FAN STITCH OVER MORE THAN ONE ROW

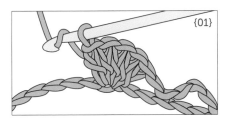

{01}

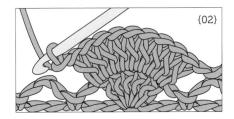

{02}

The fan stitch may begin on the very first row after the foundation chain, or it could be made on subsequent rows. Keep a tally of the stitches as they are made. Fans are often made from an uneven multiple of stitches, such as 5 or 7. Getting the number wrong on the first row could throw off the pattern on the subsequent rows.

To make a fan that increases in width over a few rows, increase as the pattern suggests into the top of the fan made on the previous row. Once again, keep a tally of the stitch count.

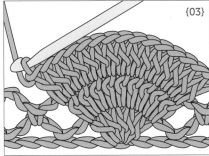

{03}

On the final row of a pattern repeat, increase as the pattern suggests into the top of the fan made on the previous row. Once again, keep a tally of the stitch count.

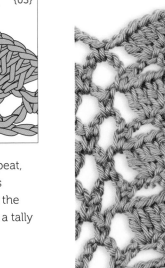

Wide fan stitch worked over more than one row.

WORKING FAN STITCH INTO A CHAIN SPACE

The pattern may ask that the group of stitches that form the fan are worked into the space created by a chain on the previous row. To work in this way, insert the hook into the gap formed by the chain on the previous round and work the stitches over the top of the chain, thus encasing it within the stitches.

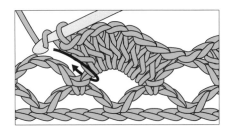

Fan stitch worked into a chain space.

Crochet edgings

Crochet fabrics have a tendency to curl. If the crochet piece is to be used as a flat fabric it may be necessary to work an edging of some sort to limit this. But edgings are not only used to stop crochet fabric from curling; they can also be used to add aesthetically pleasing effects to the crochet fabric.

CREATING A CROCHET EDGE ON A CROCHET FABRIC

Many crochet pieces will require an edging, border or fancy trim of some kind, which is created directly on the edge. The crochet edge can be worked in a matching or a contrasting yarn.

MARKING THE EDGE

If you have a set number of stitches to pick up across the edge, it is a good idea to place markers at regular intervals to ensure that you achieve an even pick-up. Measure the crochet edge. Decide how frequently a marker needs to be placed—for example, every 2" (5 cm)—and mark the edge with stitch markers, tied yarn or sewn stitches. Count how many spaces there are between the markers, then divide this number into the stitch count. For example, if there are 10 spaces and the pick-up requires 50 sts, then the calculation will be 50 divided by 10 = 5 stitches to be picked up between each marker.

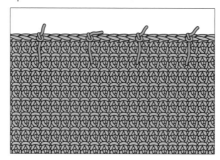

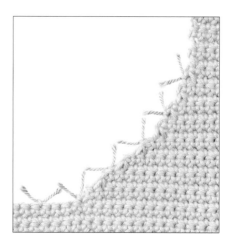

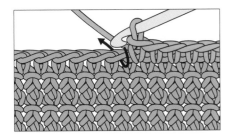

WORKING ALONG TOP (FINAL ROW) OR BOTTOM (FOUNDATION CHAIN)

Insert the hook into the center of each stitch from the front to back.

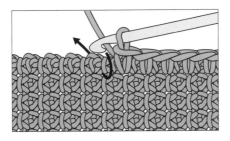

WORKING ALONG THE SIDE EDGE

Insert the hook through the work one complete stitch in from the edge from front to back.

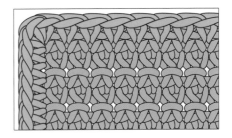

TURNING CORNERS

If you need to work an edging around a corner, then you will need to make enough stitches to achieve the turn. To do this, work 3 stitches into the corner stitch on the first row. You may also need to create more stitches or areas of chain on subsequent rows to achieve a neat corner.

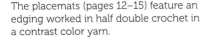

The placemats (pages 12–15) feature an edging worked in half double crochet in a contrast color yarn.

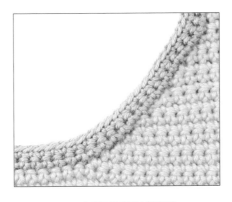

PICKING UP STITCHES USING SLIP STITCH

Working a row of slip stitch through the crochet fabric one stitch in from the edge is a neat way of creating a base for the required edging or border. The fabric edge is not bound by the stitches and will create a seam on the reverse side of the fabric.

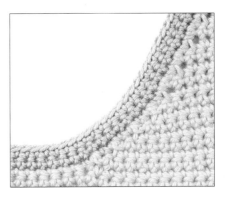

PICKING UP STITCHES USING SINGLE CROCHET

The quickest way to pick up stitches is to work single crochet around the outside of the crochet fabric one stitch in from the edge. This stitch will bind the edge of the crochet piece, so it is important that you keep the edge stitches neat and even. Once the row of single crochet is complete, it can be used as the base for the required edging or border.

SIMPLE EDGING PATTERNS

The following are some simple edging designs, which are all quite easy to create with basic crochet stitches.

SHELL EDGING

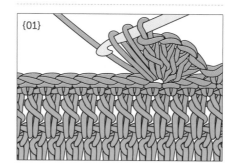

To work this edging, ensure that the foundation row is a multiple of 6 + 1. Work 1 chain, turn. Working from right to left along the edge, work 1 single crochet into the first stitch. *Skip one stitch, then work 5 double crochet into the next stitch, making sure that the stitches do not overlap.

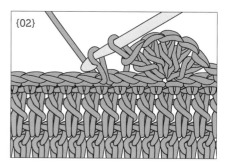

Skip 2 stitches, work a single crochet stitch into the next stitch. Continue by repeating from * to the end of the row.

Notes

This edging is worked on top of a foundation row of single crochet that is worked along the edge first. Be careful that the right side of the shell edging ends up on the right side of the fabric, by working the initial foundation row with the wrong side of the piece facing toward you.

Shells make an attractive edging for the Baby blankets (page 26); here worked into a sewn blanket stitch base stitch.

PICOT EDGING

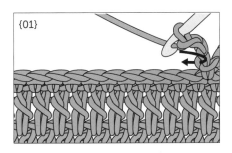

{01}

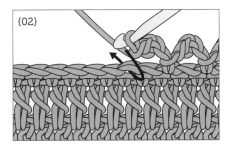

{02}

To work this edging, ensure that the foundation row is a multiple of 2. *Make 3 chains. Insert the hook into the back of the third chain from the hook (the first of the three chains made) and work a slip stitch into it.

Make 3 chains, skip one stitch. Work a slip stitch into the following stitch and repeat from * to the end of the row.

Notes

This is a simple yet very effective edging that can be worked with any number of chain stitches between the anchor stitches. This edging is worked on top of a foundation row so, as for the shell edging on the opposite page, be careful to ensure that the right sides of both the crochet fabric and the shell edging match up.

Picot edging on the shawl of the medium-size Russian Doll (page 34).

CREATING A CROCHET EDGE ON A WOVEN FABRIC

A sewn stitch such as chain stitch or blanket stitch (page 135) provides a good base for a crochet edge.

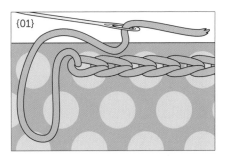

{01}

Make sure that the sewn stitches are regular and are similar in size to the crochet stitches subsequently made. It may be an idea to work a chain using the chosen yarn and hook to get an idea of stitch size.

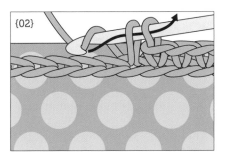

{02}

To make the crochet edge, insert the hook from front to back through the sewn stitch.

Surface crochet and embroidery

A dense crochet fabric makes a really good base for sewing stitches and simple embroidery. Such embellishments add a personal touch that can transform a plain crochet piece into something unique. Surface crochet is also a nifty way of adding detail to your work using the crochet hook instead of a sewing needle.

SEWING STITCHES

Because a tight crochet stitch, such as single crochet, produces uniform stitches in a grid-like pattern, the fabric produced can be used in much the same way as a sewing or tapestry-type canvas. For sewn stitches, it is a good idea to use a sharp sewing needle and a relatively strong thread.

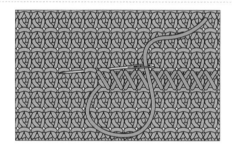

CROSS STITCH
Using cross stitch on a background of tight crochet can be a very effective way of adding adornment to the crochet piece. You may want to work to your own design or to a suitable cross stitch pattern.

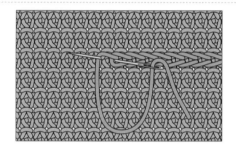

CHAIN STITCH
A sewn chain stitch has the appearance of a crochet chain, only it is bonded to the fabric. Chain stitch is great for making bold outlines or for filling in embroidered shapes. It is worked by wrapping the yarn loop around the needle before the stitch is completed.

Notes
Not all stitches are suitable for use on a crochet fabric. Very heavy embroidery can stretch the fabric and make it stiff and unwieldy. Make sure the yarn or floss you use for the embroidery is of the same or similar composition to the yarn used to make the project, or it may cause problems when washing the item. Work the stitches with the right side of the crochet facing you.

SURFACE CROCHET

The stitches produced by surface crochet look like sewn chain stitch. Using a dense and sturdy stitch for the base fabric, such as single crochet, will give you a good base for surface crochet. Using this method you will be able to make your stitches travel in any direction.

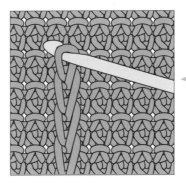

Using a contrast yarn, place a slip knot on the crochet hook. Insert the hook through the gaps between stitches. Hold the yarn to the reverse of the work. Wrap the yarn around the hook and draw through the slip knot on the hook and thus through to the front of the fabric. Repeat, continuing to draw the yarn through each stitch as required. When the design is complete, cut the yarn and pull it through the final stitch to secure.

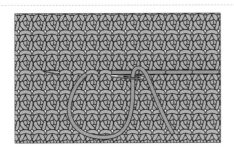

BACKSTITCH
This is another common stitch and is one that many people use for putting together crocheted or knitted garments. Backstitch is useful for creating outline details and lines.

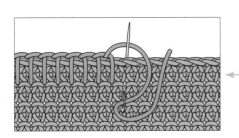

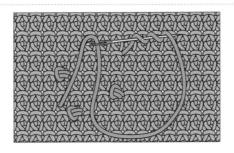

FRENCH KNOT
French knots are great for adding a little bit of extra relief work to the fabric. You can use them for details, such as the eyes on dolls or other crochet toys.

BUTTONHOLE/BLANKET STITCH
This stitch can reinforce the edge of a crochet fabric and reduces the likelihood of the fabric edge curling. It can also be used to act as a base for crochet stitches on woven or jersey fabrics (see Baby blankets, page 24).

Finishing off

{ Finishing is a very important part of crochet and could make the difference to how your finished project looks, so take time to learn some essential techniques for achieving professional results. For information on seams and joining techniques, see the next few pages.

FASTENING OFF AND SECURING YARN ENDS

Once your crochet is complete, fasten it off to stop it from unraveling, and sew or weave in yarn ends to create a neat and durable piece of crochet fabric.

Notes

It is a really good idea to sew the yarn ends in as often as possible as you work. This will mean that your work stays neater, stitches are less likely to unravel and you will not be faced with a mammoth sewing task once your crochet is complete.

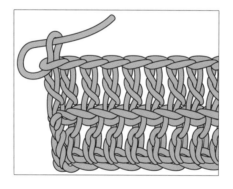

TO FASTEN OFF THE CROCHET THREAD ON FINAL STITCH

When the final stitch of the crochet piece is completed, slip the loop from the crochet hook and cut the yarn, leaving a tail end of about 4" (10 cm). Thread the cut end of yarn through the loop from the back to front. Pull on the yarn to tighten the stitch.

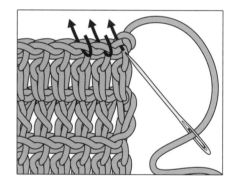

TO SEW IN A YARN END AT THE TOP EDGE

Thread a large tapestry needle with the yarn end and sew through the reverse side of each stitch of the last row of crochet. Sew for about 2" (5 cm) then make an extra stitch into the final back loop. Trim the remaining yarn, being careful not to cut too close to the final stitch.

BLOCKING

Blocking is the term used to describe the laying out of the crochet piece prior to sewing it together. It involves pinning a piece of crocheted fabric to the correct size, and then either steaming it with an iron or moistening with cold water, depending on the fiber content of the yarn.

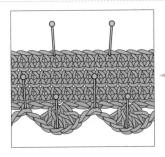

It may be necessary to pin the item down if it is prone to curling or if it needs to be slightly stretched back into size or shape. Pieces to be joined together should be blocked with right side facing down and secured using large-headed pins. If necessary, ease the fabric to achieve the correct measurements. Leave to dry away from direct sunlight or a heat source and turn occasionally.

Notes

If many motifs have been made over a period of time they may be slightly different sizes due to varying gauge at different times of working, but blocking and pressing can correct such minor variations. When working with lots of motifs that are all supposed to be identical, draw a template in waterproof pen on a piece of fabric and pin the motifs out using the template as a guide.

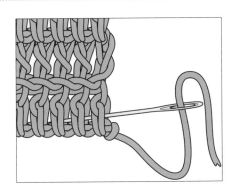

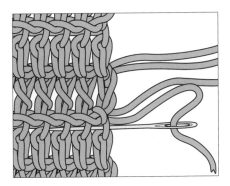

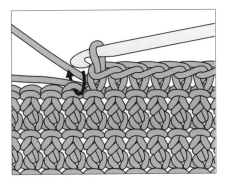

TO SEW IN A YARN END AT THE LOWER EDGE

Thread a large tapestry needle with the yarn end and sew through the core of each stitch of the first row of crochet. Sew for about 2" (5 cm), then bring the yarn through the work and make an extra stitch into the back loop of a stitch. Trim the remaining yarn, being careful not to cut too close to the final stitch.

TO SEW IN YARN ENDS ON A STRIPE PATTERN

Work using either of the two above methods, being careful that the yarn ends are not showing through to the right side of the work.

Notes

To avoid the need to sew yarn ends in, you can choose to work your next row of crochet over the top of a yarn end, thus trapping it within the formation of the stitch.

TO CROCHET OVER YARN ENDS

Work to the position of the yarn tails and prepare to work the stitch of your choice. Hold the tail end of the yarn in line with the top of the previous row, to the left of the stitches just worked. Insert the hook into the following stitch position and under the tail end of yarn. Complete the stitch, trapping the yarn tail within it. Repeat for about 2" (5 cm). Trim the remaining yarn.

SEWN SEAMS

You can use a variety of sewn stitches to join your crochet pieces. Sew all yarn ends in neatly first and block pieces if necessary before assembling them. Use a large tapestry needle to stitch with.

Notes

When working with the wrong side facing, remember to regularly check your stitching on the right side for any mistakes that will show. You can use pins or markers to ensure that you match the seam correctly.

BACKSTITCH SEAM

Hold the pieces together with right sides of the work facing inward. Work a row of backstitch from right to left, making sure the stitches run in a straight line. The sewn seam can be one or two stitches in from the edge, depending on which looks neater.

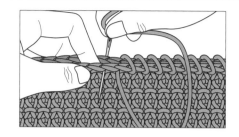

OVERSEWN SEAM

Try to keep the stitch size even and regular, otherwise stitching can look messy on the right side. Hold the two crochet pieces together with right sides facing inward. Place your left index finger between the two pieces to open the seam and make small sewn stitches around both edges to join. Where possible, join stitch for stitch.

CROCHET SEAMS

Some crochet stitches can also be used to join crochet pieces once complete. This can produce a firm and well-defined edge as can be seen in the Sunburst motif cushion (pages 48–51).

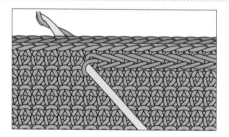

SLIP STITCH SEAM

This is the crochet equivalent of chain stitch. Hold the crochet pieces together, right sides of the work facing inward. Work a row of stitches from right to left by inserting the hook through each stitch and catching the yarn held at the back of the work. Draw the yarn through the fabric and create a slip stitch. Make sure the stitches run in a straight line.

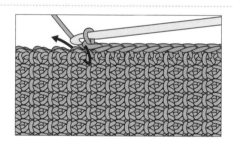

SINGLE CROCHET ON A SIDE SEAM

Hold the two crochet pieces together, right sides facing inward. Place your left index finger between the two pieces to open the seam. Insert the hook through a stitch on the front piece, then through its corresponding stitch on the back piece. Draw the yarn through from the reverse of the work and complete a stitch. Where possible, join stitch for stitch.

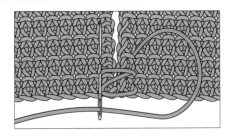

MATTRESS STITCH SEAM
This almost invisible sewn seam is done with the fabrics laying flat and face up. Do not start this at the very beginning of the seam, but start a few rows or stitches in from the end of the work. Leave a long tail end of yarn at the beginning and use it to finish off the first section of the seam once the majority of its length is complete.

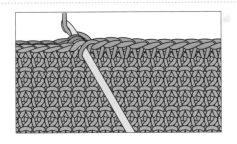

SINGLE CROCHET ON A TOP SEAM
Crocheting along a top seam is quick and easy; where possible, join stitch for stitch. If the stitch count differs between the pieces, decrease by working stitches together where needed. Hold the two crochet pieces together, right sides facing inward and the top seams running parallel to each other. Place your left index finger between the two pieces to open the

Lay the pieces flat, right sides facing. Working one stitch in from the edge of the left-hand piece, insert the needle through the work from front to back about four rows or stitches up from the lower end of the seam. Bring the needle through to the front of the work one stitch up. Insert the needle into the corresponding stitch on the right-hand piece from front to back, then out to the front of the work one stitch higher. From the front, insert the needle into the stitch on the left-hand piece where the yarn from the previous stitch emerges. Bring the needle back through to the front of the work one stitch higher. Repeat, tightening the sewing every few stitches.

Notes
Often your crochet pattern will specify what sort of seam to use, but not always. Experiment with the different types—sometimes you will want a near-invisible seam, but some projects will suit a more obvious and defined seam.

seam. Insert the hook through a stitch on the front piece, then through its corresponding stitch on the back piece. Draw the yarn through from the reverse of the work and complete a stitch.

JOINING CIRCLES AND BLOCKS TOGETHER

When joining motifs together there are a few specific techniques you can use that will give a better result.

JOINING CIRCULAR MOTIFS

Because circular motifs—or motifs with very curved edges—do not have straight sides, they are not as easy to join together as angular shapes, such as squares and triangles. The best way to join circular shapes is to work a few sewn stitches in a matching yarn just where the circles touch.

Notes
If you find that joining the circles together causes them to distort a little, try blocking them into shape again.

JOINING FOUR SQUARE MOTIFS WITH SEWN STITCHES

For a neat join, work your sewn stitches through just one loop of the stitch. For a stronger seam, work your stitches through both loops.

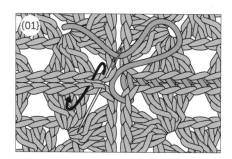

Join the first two blocks using the preferred sewing stitch. At the end of the straight edge, position two more blocks. Thread the sewing needle through the first stitch on both of the blocks in order to join all four together. Continue to sew blocks together in this way to end.

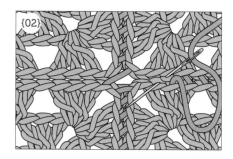

Turn the work so that the open seam is horizontal. Use the chosen sewing stitch to work along this seam to end.

JOINING FOUR SQUARE MOTIFS WITH SLIP STITCH

You can make a nice feature of the slip stitch by working it in a contrast color.

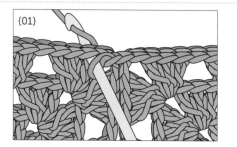

Join the first two blocks using slip stitch. At the end of the straight edge, position two more blocks. Insert the hook through the first stitch on both of the blocks in order to join all four together. Continue to crochet blocks together in this way to end.

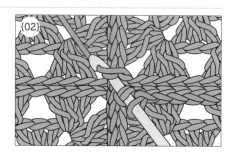

Turn the work so that the open seam is horizontal. Use the chosen crochet stitch to work along this seam to end. Where the blocks meet, carry the yarn across the ridge created by the seam and pull gently in order to work a tight, strong stitch.

JOINING MOTIFS AS YOU WORK

Depending on the chosen motif, it may be possible to join the crochet pieces to one another as you complete the final round of each one. It is a good idea to piece the motifs together in long strips first, which can then be joined to each other using a further row of stitching.

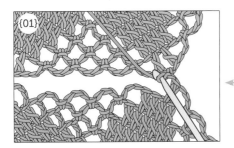

Complete one motif. Work the second motif until you reach the final round. Work according to the pattern down one side of the motif. At the corner, line up the first motif with the second one and work a stitch into the corner space of both motifs simultaneously.

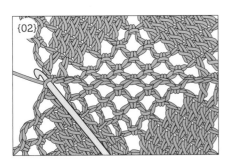

Work according to the pattern around the second motif, working joining stitches with areas of chain in between, where possible, in order to attach the first motif.

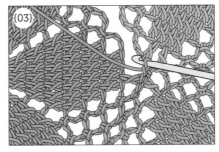

Finish the final round of the second motif. Join further motifs in the same way.

BUTTON FASTENINGS

Choose your buttons before you begin making your buttonholes or button loops, so the hole or loop can be made to fit the button rather than the other way round. After making the first one, check it fits the button correctly before making more; if not you can adjust the size. It may not be necessary to remake an incorrect first buttonhole or loop—if it is too tight it may stretch a little, if too loose, sew a stitch across the end.

A button loop makes a good alternative to a buttonhole as can be seen on the iPad cover (pages 70–72).

MAKING A BUTTONHOLE WITHIN A PIECE

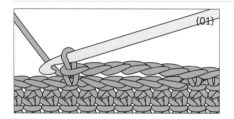

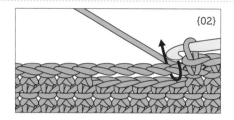

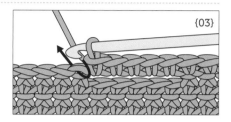

Work to the position of the required buttonhole. Decide how many stitches to skip and make a chain to the same length. Secure the chain in place by working a stitch into the next stitch. Continue along the row, making chains to create subsequent holes where required.

On the return row, work stitches around the chain that was made on the previous row. Make the same number of stitches around the chain as were used to make the chain.

At the end of the chain, work a stitch into the next stitch of the row. Continue along the row, working into the spaces made by each chain on the previous row.

MAKING BUTTON LOOPS

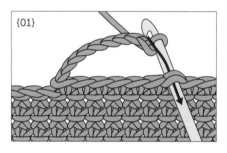

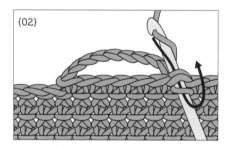

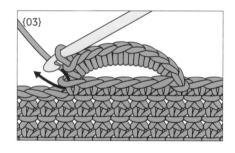

With wrong side facing, first work to the position of the required button loop. Place a stitch marker in the last stitch, then work a few more stitches. Make a chain long enough to go over the button, remembering the loop will stretch slightly. Slip the yarn loop from the hook and thread the hook through the marked stitch from front to back. Place the loop back on the hook and draw through the stitch.

Insert the hook back through the same stitch. Wrap the yarn around the hook and draw through to the front.

Work enough stitches around the chain to fill the loop. Work the final stitch of the loop into the stitch at the base of the chain, as shown by the arrow in the illustration.

Notes
The illustrations show how to make a horizontal button loop. It is also possible to make a vertical button loop as on the iPad cover (pages 70–72).

{04}
Insert the hook into the next stitch beyond the button loop and continue along the row, making subsequent loops where required.

INDEX

FIND MORE UNIQUE HANDMADE INSPIRATION
from MOLLIE MAKES, available at Interweave

MOLLIE MAKES CHRISTMAS
Living and Loving a Handmade Holiday
ISBN 978-1-62033-101-9 | $12.95

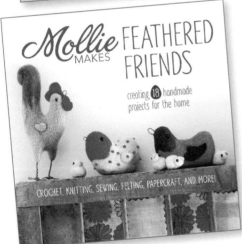

MOLLIE MAKES FEATHERED FRIENDS
Creating 18 Handmade Projects for the Home
ISBN 978-1-59668-775-2 | $12.95

First published in the United States in 2013 by
Interweave
A division of F+W Media, Inc.
201 East Fourth Street
Loveland, CO 80537
interweave.com

© 2013 Collins & Brown

ISBN 978-1-62033-095-1

Library of Congress Cataloging-in-Publication Data not available at time of printing.

10 9 8 7 6 5 4 3 2

Manufactured in China by
1010 Printing International Limited.

Get your copy at your favorite retailer or at www.interweavestore.com.

PUBLISHER'S ACKNOWLEDGMENTS

This book would not have been possible without the input of all our fantastic crafty contributors. We would also like to thank Cheryl Brown, who has done a great job of pulling everything together, Nicola Hodgson for her meticulous checking, and Sophie Martin for her design work. Thanks to Kuo Kang Chen for his excellent illustrations and to Rachel Whiting for her photography.

And of course, thanks must go to the fantastic team at *Mollie Makes* for all their help, in particular Jane Toft, Lara Watson, and Katherine Raderecht.